# TENNESSEE WILLIAMS

WORLD DRAMATISTS / *General Editor: Lina Mainiero*
*In the same series:*

| | |
|---|---|
| Edward Albee | *Ronald Hayman* |
| Jean Anouilh | *Louis J. Falb* |
| Samuel Beckett | *Ronald Hayman* |
| Bertolt Brecht | *Karl H. Schoeps* |
| Georg Büchner | *William C. Reeve* |
| Pedro Calderón de la | |
| Barca | *Heinz Gerstinger* |
| Anton Chekhov | *Siegfried Melchinger* |
| Euripides | *Siegfried Melchinger* |
| Georges Feydeau | *Leonard C. Pronko* |
| Carlo Goldoni | *Heinz Riedt* |
| Oliver Goldsmith and | |
| Richard Sheridan | *Marlies K. Danziger* |
| Henrik Ibsen | *Hans Georg Meyer* |
| Eugène Ionesco | *Ronald Hayman* |
| Christopher Marlowe | *Gerald Pinciss* |
| Arthur Miller | *Ronald Hayman* |
| Molière | *Gertrud Mander* |
| Sean O'Casey | *Doris daRin* |
| John Osborne | *Ronald Hayman* |
| Harold Pinter | *Ronald Hayman* |
| Luigi Pirandello | *Renate Matthaei* |
| Friedrich Schiller | *Charles E. Passage* |
| Arthur Schnitzler | *Reinhard Urbach* |
| Shakespeare's Histories | *George J. Becker* |
| Shakespeare's Tragedies | *Phyllis Rackin* |
| Bernard Shaw | *Pat M. Carr* |
| Sophocles | *Siegfried Melchinger* |
| August Strindberg | *Gunnar Ollén* |
| Lope de Vega | |
| and Spanish Drama | *Heinz Gerstinger* |
| Arnold Wesker | *Ronald Hayman* |
| Tennessee Williams | *Felicia Hardison Londré* |
| William Butler Yeats | *Anthony Bradley* |

WORLD DRAMATISTS

# TENNESSEE

# WILLIAMS

FELICIA HARDISON LONDRÉ

**WITH HALFTONE ILLUSTRATIONS**

FREDERICK UNGAR PUBLISHING CO.

New York

*Copyright © 1979 by Frederick Ungar Publishing Co., Inc.*
*Printed in the United States of America*
*Designed by Edith Fowler*

Library of Congress Cataloging in Publication Data
Londré, Felicia Hardison, 1941–
   Tennessee Williams.
   Bibliography: p.
   Includes index.
   1. Williams, Tennessee, 1911–   —Criticism
and interpretation.
PS3545.I5365Z745     812'.5'4    79–4830
ISBN 0–8044–2539–6

# CONTENTS

# CHRONOLOGY

1911            March 26. Thomas Lanier Williams is
                born in Columbus, Mississippi, the sec-
                ond child, first son, of Cornelius Coffin
                ("C.C.") Williams, a traveling shoe sales-
                man, and Edwina ("Miss Edwina") Dakin
                Williams. Because of his father's frequent
                absence, his mother and sister Rose (b.
                1909) live with his maternal grandparents
                Reverend and Mrs. Walter E. Dakin
                (Grandfather and "Grand") in the rec-
                tory of St. Paul's Episcopal Church.

1914–1918       Reverend Dakin and extended family
                live one year in Nashville, a few months
                in Canton, Mississippi, and then settle in
                Clarksdale, Mississippi, eighty miles south
                of Memphis. In Clarksdale, a nearly fatal
                attack of diphtheria leaves Tom an in-
                valid for almost two years, during which
                time he relies heavily on the life of the
                imagination, fueled by the attentions of
                his mother, grandmother, sister, and
                Ozzie. The latter is a black nursemaid
                and teller of supernatural tales, who lives
                with the family until Tom is six.

1918 July. The Williamses move to St. Louis, where "C.C." is now branch sales manager for International Shoe Company.

1919 January. Dakin Williams is born. Tom returns to live with his grandparents in Clarksdale for one year while his mother recovers from influenza.

1920–1929 "Nine years in limbo" is how Williams remembers growing up in St. Louis, where the family lives in a succession of eight different apartments. His parents quarrel constantly; Miss Edwina is frequently ill; and Tom cowers before the coarse, violent-tempered father who taunts him with the nickname "Miss Nancy."

1922 Miss Edwina buys Tom a second-hand typewriter. He begins writing stories as a "compensation" for his discovery of snobbery in "middle American life." Hazel Kramer becomes his closest childhood friend, a companionship which lasts eleven years.

1927 April. He wins third prize of five dollars for his entry in an essay contest, "Can a Good Wife be a Good Sport?," sponsored by *Smart Set* magazine.

He wins ten dollars from Loew's State Theater in St. Louis for the best review of the movie *Stella Dallas*.

He writes "The Vengeance of Nitocris," his first published story (*Weird Tales*, June 1928), for which he is paid thirty-five dollars.

1928 Grandfather Dakin takes him on a tour of Europe.

1929 Williams enters the University of Missouri, Columbia. He writes a proposal of marriage to Hazel Kramer. He joins ATO fraternity. His play, *Beauty Is the Word*, wins honorable mention in the University of Missouri dramatic arts contest.

1931      He fails ROTC at the University of Missouri. "C.C." refuses to allow him to return there in the fall.

1931–1935 Williams works days in the Continental Shoemakers branch of International Shoe Company for sixty-five dollars a month, and spends his nights writing stories.

1933      He wins first prize in a St. Louis Writers Guild contest for amateurs with his story, "Stella for Star."

1935      February. Hazel Kramer marries Terence McCabe.

March. Williams is hospitalized briefly for a heart condition and is released from his shoe company job.

Rose's mental disturbances begin to be apparent.

Summer. Williams recuperates at Grandfather and Grand's house in Memphis. The Garden Players of the Rose Arbor Theater in Memphis produce his play, *Cairo! Shanghai! Bombay!*

1936      September. He enrolls at Washington University in St. Louis. He and Clark Mills McBurney run a "literary factory" in McBurney's cellar.

October. Webster Groves Theater Guild presents Williams's play *The Magic Tower*, which had won their one-act playwriting contest. He is awarded an engraved silver cake plate.

November. The Mummers of St. Louis present Williams's *Headlines*, which they had asked him to write as a curtain-raiser to be performed with Irwin Shaw's *Bury the Dead*. Williams is not given program credit for his play.

He wins first prize of twenty-five dollars in the senior division of an original verse contest sponsored by the Wednesday Club of St. Louis.

1937      He enters *Me, Vashya!* in a Washington University playwriting contest, but does not win. Disappointed, he lets his grades fall.

June. He is dropped from Washington University.

September. He enters the University of Iowa.

The Mummers of St. Louis produce *The Fugitive Kind* and *Candles to the Sun,* his first two full-length plays.

He writes two more full-length plays in Professor E.C. Mabie's playwriting class: *Spring Storm* and *Not about Nightingales.*

A prefrontal lobotomy is performed on Rose without Williams's advance knowledge of his parents' decision.

1938      Summer. He completes his B.A. degree at the University of Iowa. He goes to Chicago in hopes of joining the WPA Writers' Project, but is turned down.

1938–1939      Williams lives in the French Quarter of New Orleans, working as a waiter by day and becoming acquainted with low life at night.

He first uses the name "Tennessee" on a story published in *Story* magazine, "The Field of Blue Children."

He submits his four full-length plays and a group of one-acts entitled *American Blues* to a contest sponsored by the Group Theater in New York for young writers under twenty-five; he gives his birth date as 1914.

He travels to California with a friend. They live on a pigeon ranch ten miles out of Culver City, where he works at Clark's Bootery. He receives $100 prize money from the Group Theater contest for *American Blues*. Williams and his friend use the money for a bicycle trip to Mexico and spend the rest of the summer working on a squab ranch near Laguna Beach, "the happiest summer of [his] life."

Audrey Wood becomes his agent and sends him a Rockefeller Fellowship application form.

He returns to St. Louis via Taos, New Mexico, where he meets the widow of D.H. Lawrence. In St. Louis, he works on a new full-length play, *Battle of Angels*.

December. Williams is notified of winning a thousand-dollar grant from the Rockefeller Foundation. He goes to New York.

1940      January. He enrolls in a seminar in advanced playwriting conducted by Teresa Helburn and John Gassner at the New School for Social Research. He meets Donald Windham, with whom he is to correspond for twenty years.

February. The New School for Social Research stages Williams's one-act play, *The Long Goodbye*.

April. *Battle of Angels* is optioned by the Theater Guild.

Summer. Williams goes to Provincetown to work on revisions. He meets Kip, a friend to whose memory Williams remains devoted long after his premature death in 1944 at age twenty-six.

August. Williams travels to Mexico to get

over a break with Kip, stays a week at the
YMCA in Mexico City, then settles at the
Hotel Costa Verde in Acapulco, where
he encounters a party of Nazi Germans
resembling those he ultimately uses in
*The Night of the Iguana*. He begins work
on *Stairs to the Roof*.

December 30. The Theater Guild produc-
tion of *Battle of Angels*, directed by
Margaret Webster, opens at the Wilbur
Theater in Boston; it closes there on
January 11. Williams is told that the
Theater Guild will consider any revision
of the play for the next season.

1941    January. He undergoes the first of four
cataract operations on his left eye, then
winters in Key West while working on the
*Battle of Angels* rewrite.

Williams is granted an additional $500.00
from the Rockefeller committee to enable
him to write a new play. When that runs
out, he works as a night-shift elevator
operator at the San Jacinto Hotel in New
York.

Summer. He lives in Provincetown and
writes *I Rise in Flame, Cried the Phoenix*.

1942    March. Williams begins collaboration
with Donald Windham on a dramatization of D.H. Lawrence's short story, "You
Touched Me."

May. Williams submits a revised *Battle of
Angels* to the Theater Guild. The New
School for Social Research presents *This
Property Is Condemned*.

June–August. He lives in Macon, Georgia,
working on *You Touched Me!*

August. The Theater Guild rejects the revised *Battle of Angels*.

August–October. Williams works as a teletype operator for $120 a month in the U.S. Engineers Office, Jacksonville, Florida.

Winter. In New York, Williams works at Valesca Gert's Beggars' Bar "as a poetry-reciting waiter, wearing a black eyepatch after another cataract operation."

1943    *You Touched Me!* is turned down by all potential Broadway producers.

April. At his mother's house in St. Louis, he begins work on *The Gentleman Caller* (later *The Glass Menagerie*).

May. He works as an usher in the Strand Theater in New York for $17.00 a week. Audrey Wood gets him a contract with MGM as a scriptwriter for $250 a week.

At MGM, Williams works on a screenplay for Lana Turner, then a scenario about Billy the Kid. On his own time, he continues work on *The Gentleman Caller.*

August–September. The studio exercises the six-weeks' lay-off clause in Williams's contract "in retaliation for [his] unwillingness to undertake another stupid assignment."

October. *You Touched Me!* is presented in Cleveland, Ohio, directed by Margo Jones.

November 29–December 5. The Margo Jones production of *You Touched Me!* is presented in the Playbox at Pasadena Playhouse.

December. He visits Frieda Lawrence in Taos en route to St. Louis for Christmas. Grand dies in St. Louis after Williams arrives there.

1944    March. He returns to New York.

May. He receives a $1,000 award from the National Institute of Arts and Letters for

*Battle of Angels* and for his one-act plays. June–August. He spends the summer in Provincetown and finishes *The Glass Menagerie.*

December 26. *The Glass Menagerie* opens in Chicago, directed by Eddie Dowling and Margo Jones. Despite poor attendance at first, Chicago critics keep the play alive until it becomes a recognized triumph. Williams begins getting $1,000 a week in royalties on it.

1945    March 25–April 7. *Stairs to the Roof* is presented at Pasadena Playhouse. It is revived in 1947, February 26–March 9, at the same theater, directed by Margo Jones.

March 31. *The Glass Menagerie* opens at the Playhouse in New York. Williams signs over half of the rights to Miss Edwina. The play wins the New York Drama Critics' Circle Award, the Sidney Howard Memorial Award of $1,500 presented by the Playwright's Company, the Donaldson Award sponsored by *Billboard,* and the "Sign" Award from *National Catholic* magazine. It is revived in New York in 1956, 1965, and 1975.

May. Williams undergoes another eye operation, then travels to Mexico. There, he works on *The Poker Night* (later *A Streetcar Named Desire*), *Summer and Smoke*, and some stories.

September 25. *You Touched Me!* opens at the Booth Theater in New York. Critics compare it unfavorably to *The Glass Menagerie*, and it runs only until January 5.

1946    *The Glass Menagerie* is chosen for performance at the Roosevelt birthday celebration at the National Theater, Washington, D.C.

May. En route from St. Louis to Taos, New Mexico, he suffers severe abdominal pains, which are falsely diagnosed in Alva, Oklahoma, and in Wichita. In Taos, an operation saves his life, but marks the beginning of a three-year period of living with the constant fear of imminent death.

Summer. He lives in a rented cottage on Nantucket, where Carson McCullers works on her dramatization of *The Member of the Wedding* and Williams works on *Summer and Smoke*.

Later in the year, Williams is hospitalized in New York, "recovering from his summer on Nantucket with Carson McCullers," according to Donald Windham.

1947    Williams and his grandfather Dakin live in Key West while Williams works on *The Poker Night*.

July 11. *Summer and Smoke* opens at Theater '47, Dallas, Texas, directed by Margo Jones.

December 3. *A Streetcar Named Desire* opens at the Barrymore Theater in New York, directed by Elia Kazan. It wins the New York Drama Critics' Circle Award, the Pulitzer Prize, and the Donaldson Award, the first play ever to win all three awards. Williams gives the Pulitzer Prize money to the University of Missouri for a graduate journalism scholarship. The play is revived in New York in 1956 and in 1973.

Miss Edwina orders "C.C." out of the St. Louis house; Dakin Williams, now an attorney, draws up the contract of separation. Miss Edwina never sees her husband again.

1948    January. After a visit to Paris, Williams makes his first trip to Italy and likes Rome well enough to take an apartment there. He stays in Rome through June, and returns, via London and Paris, to the United States in August.

*One Arm and Other Stories* is published.

Fall. Williams begins his fourteen-year liaison with Frank Merlo.

October 6, 1948. *Summer and Smoke* opens at the Music Box in New York, directed by Margo Jones. It closes before Christmas.

1949    January–June. Williams lives in Rome, with side trips to North Africa, London, and Paris.

November. Williams lives in Key West and works on *The Rose Tattoo*.

1950    *The Roman Spring of Mrs. Stone*, a novel, is published.

Warner Brothers releases a film version of *The Glass Menagerie*, screenplay by Williams and Paul Berneis, directed by Irving Rapper.

December. *The Rose Tattoo* opens at the Erlanger Theater in Chicago.

1951    February 3. *The Rose Tattoo* opens at the Martin Beck Theater in New York, directed by Daniel Mann. It wins the Antoinette Perry (Tony) Award for Best Play.

Warner Brothers releases a film version of *A Streetcar Named Desire*, screenplay by Williams and Oscar Saul, directed by Elia Kazan.

1952    *Summer and Smoke* is revived by José

Quintero at the Circle in the Square, with Geraldine Page as Alma.

1953    March 19. *Camino Real* opens at the National Theater in New York, directed by Elia Kazan. Reviews are savage and the play closes after sixty performances. After the opening Williams leaves for Key West to work on revisions. The play is revived in January 1970 at the Vivian Beaumont Theater, directed by Milton Katselas, to favorable critical response.

April–May. Williams directs the original production of Donald Windham's play, *The Starless Air*, in Houston. Williams is signed to direct the play in New York for the Theater Guild, but he sails for Europe in June.

1954    *Hard Candy*; *A Book of Stories* is published.

1955    March 24. *Cat on a Hot Tin Roof* opens at the Morosco Theater in New York, directed by Elia Kazan. It wins the New York Drama Critics' Circle Award and the Pulitzer Prize and becomes his longest running play. However, Williams is disappointed with the opening night performance and leaves for Rome shortly afterward. The play is revived in September 1974 at the ANTA Theater in New York, with a rewritten third act.

Summer. While traveling in Europe, Williams works on the screenplay for *Baby Doll* (based on two earlier short plays, *27 Wagons Full of Cotton* and *The Unsatisfactory Supper; or, The Long Stay Cut Short*). From this summer on, he writes "usually under artificial stimulants, aside from the true stimulant of [his] deep-rooted need to continue to write."

Grandfather Dakin dies at age 97.

Paramount releases the film version of *The Rose Tattoo*, screenplay by Williams and Hal Kanter, directed by Daniel Mann.

1956    *In the Winter of Cities*, a collection of poems, is published.

Warner Brothers releases the film, *Baby Doll*, original screenplay by Williams, directed by Elia Kazan.

March 21. *Orpheus Descending* (based upon the earlier *Battle of Angels*) opens at the Martin Beck Theater in New York, directed by Harold Clurman. It closes after sixty-eight performances.

Williams begins psychiatric analysis.

Cornelius Coffin Williams dies in a Knoxville hotel room. Williams and his brother Dakin both attend the funeral.

1958    January 7. *Garden District* (two short plays, *Something Unspoken* and *Suddenly Last Summer*) opens at the York playhouse, off-Broadway, directed by Herbert Machiz.

April 16. Kraft Television Theater present *Moony's Kid Don't Cry*, *The Last of My Solid Gold Watches*, and *This Property Is Condemned*.

MGM releases the film version of *Cat on a Hot Tin Roof*, screenplay by Richard Brooks and James Poe, produced by Lawrence Weingarten.

1959    March 10. *Sweet Bird of Youth* opens at the Martin Beck Theater, directed by Elia Kazan. It had been first produced in Coral Gables, Florida, in 1956. It is revived in December 1974 in New York.

Columbia Pictures releases the film version of *Suddenly, Last Summer*, screenplay by Williams and Gore Vidal, directed by Joseph L. Mankiewicz.

1960     Early, short version of *The Night of the Inguana* is presented at the Festival of Two Worlds, Spoleto, Italy.

November 10. *Period of Adjustment* opens at the Helen Hayes Theater in New York, directed by George Roy Hill. It had been first produced at the Coconut Grove Playhouse in Miami, codirected by Williams.

United Artists releases *The Fugitive Kind,* a film version of *Orpheus Descending*, screenplay by Williams and Meade Roberts, directed by Sidney Lumet.

1961     Paramount releases a film version of *Summer and Smoke*, screenplay by James Poe and Meade Roberts, directed by Peter Glenville.

Warner Brothers releases a film version of *The Roman Spring of Mrs. Stone*, screenplay by Gavin Lambert, based upon the novel by Williams, directed by José Quintero.

Williams accompanies the pre-Broadway tour of *The Night of the Iguana* to Rochester, Detroit, Cleveland, and Chicago. In Detroit, he has a close brush with death due to dog bites on both ankles.

December 29. *The Night of the Iguana* opens at the Royale Theater, directed by Frank Corsaro. It wins the New York Drama Critics' Circle Award. It is revived in 1976 in New York.

1962     MGM releases a film version of *Sweet Bird of Youth*, screenplay by Richard Brooks, directed by Richard Brooks.

June. A one-act version of *The Milk*

*Train Doesn't Stop Here Anymore* is presented at the Festival of Two Worlds in Spoleto, Italy.

MGM releases a film version of *Period of Adjustment,* screenplay by Isobel Lennart, directed by George Roy Hill.

1963   January 16. First expanded version of *The Milk Train Doesn't Stop Here Anymore* opens at the Morosco Theater in New York. Revised versions are presented at the Barter Theater, Abingdon, Virginia, in fall 1963, at the Brooks Atkinson Theater in New York in January 1964, and at the Encore Theater in San Francisco in July 1965.

Fall. Frank Merlo dies of cancer.

Williams goes into a long period of depression and isolation, broken only by his work and occasional productions of his plays. He refers to the 1960s as his "Stoned Age."

1964   MGM releases a film version of *The Night of the Iguana,* screenplay by Anthony Veiller and John Huston, directed by John Huston.

*Eccentricities of a Nightingale* (based upon the earlier play, *Summer and Smoke*) is published. It is not produced on Broadway until 1976.

1966   February 22. *Slapstick Tragedy* (two short plays, *The Mutilated* and *The Gnädiges Fräulein*) opens at the Longacre Theater in New York, directed by Alan Schneider. It closes after seven performances.

Seven Arts releases a film version of *This Property Is Condemned,* screenplay by Francis Ford Coppola, Fred Coe, and Edith Sommer, suggested by the one-act play by Williams, directed by Sydney Pollack.

1967    *The Knightly Quest,* a novella and four short stories, is published.

*The Two-Character Play* is produced by the Hampstead Theater Club in London. (See July 1971 for subsequent revisions and productions of this play.)

1968    March 27. *The Seven Descents of Myrtle,* directed by José Quintero, opens at the Ethel Barrymore Theater in New York and is reviewed unfavorably. It is published later that year as *Kingdom of Earth.*

Universal Pictures releases *Boom,* a film version of *The Milk Train Doesn't Stop Here Anymore,* screenplay by Williams, directed by Joseph Losey.

1969    January 6. Williams is baptized into the Roman Catholic faith in the Church of St. Mary Star of the Sea, Key West, Florida.

May 11. *In the Bar of a Tokyo Hotel* opens at the Eastside Playhouse in New York, directed by Herbert Machiz. Reviews are unfavorable; Williams flees to Tokyo with Anne Meacham, who played Miriam in the production. He returns to Key West in late summer.

May 21. Williams receives the Gold Medal for Drama from the American Academy of Arts and Letters.

Williams goes through a period of convulsions, delirium, and a "silent coronary" while confined at Barnacle Hospital in St. Louis. He is released, after a three-month stay, in time for the Christmas holidays.

1970    Williams travels to Bangkok to undergo an operation for gynecomastia.

1971     July 8. *Out Cry* opens at the Ivanhoe
         Theater in Chicago. A revised version
         opens at the Lyceum Theater in New York
         on March 1, 1973, directed by Peter Glen-
         ville. A further-revised version, again en-
         titled *The Two-Character Play*, opens at
         the Quaigh Theater in New York on
         August 14, 1975, directed by Bill Lentsch.
         Williams breaks off his professional rela-
         tions with Audrey Wood and is subse-
         quently represented by Bill Barnes.

1972     April 2. *Small Craft Warnings* opens at
         the Truck and Warehouse Theater in
         New York, directed by Richard Altman.
         The production is later relocated to the
         New Theater. Williams makes his acting
         debut in the role of Doc for the first five
         performances in the new location, begin-
         ning June 6. He takes up the role again
         later in the run as a means of drawing
         more people to the play.

1973     December 9. Williams receives the first
         centennial medal of Cathedral Church of
         St. John the Divine during Sunday-in-
         Advent services entitled "The Artist as
         Prophet."

1974     *Eight Mortal Ladies Possessed*, a collec-
         tion of short stories, is published.

1975     February 20. Williams receives the Na-
         tional Arts Club's gold medal for litera-
         ture.
         May. *Moise and the World of Reason*, a
         novel, is published.
         June 18. *The Red Devil Battery Sign*
         opens at the Shubert Theater in Boston.
         It closes ten days later. It is rewritten and
         produced in Vienna in February 1976.
         October. Tennessee Williams's *Memoirs*
         are published.

1976    January. *The Demolition Downtown* is produced at the Carnaby Street Theater in London.

January 20. *This Is (An Entertainment)* opens at the American Conservatory Theater in San Francisco, directed by Allen Fletcher. After the Boston closing of *Red Devil Battery Sign*, Williams had decided that his next play should open as far from New York as possible. Williams spends a month in residence with the ACT Company during the rehearsal period. Reviewers fail to acknowledge that the play is a "work in progress," and the response is mixed.

January 26. *27 Wagons Full of Cotton* opens on a double bill with Arthur Miller's one-act *A Memory of Two Mondays* at the Playhouse in New York, directed by Arvin Brown.

November 23. *Eccentricities of a Nightingale* opens at the Morosco Theater in New York, directed by Edwin Sherin.

December 6. PBS Television broadcasts "Tennessee Williams' South," a documentary special on the man and his work. *Tennessee Williams' Letters to Donald Windham, 1940–1965* are published.

1977    May 11. *Vieux Carré* opens at the St. James Theater in New York, directed by Arthur Allen Seidelman.

*Androgyne, Mon Amour,* a collection of poems, is published.

1978    January 19–February 4. *Tiger Tail* is produced at the Alliance Theater, Atlanta Memorial Arts Center, Atlanta, Georgia, directed by Harry Rasky.

June 1–11. *Crève Coeur* is produced at the Dock Street Theatre, Charleston, South

Carolina, for the Spoleto U.S.A. Festival, directed by Keith Hack.

*Where I Live; Selected Essays* by Tennessee Williams is published.

1979    January 21. *A Lovely Sunday for Crève Coeur,* a revised version of *Crève Coeur,* opens at the Hudson Guild Theatre in New York, directed by Keith Hack.

AUTHOR'S NOTE: Since Tennessee Williams may spend years rewriting and polishing a play, there frequently are textual variants in the published versions, most notably between the acting editions and the presumably definitive texts published by New Directions. Except as indicated in the Bibliography, the latter editions were used for this study.

The full-length plays are discussed in order of their production in New York, which was almost without exception the order of their composition. The one-act plays are discussed in order of publication or of their arrangement within the three collections of short plays: *American Blues*, *Twenty-seven Wagons Full of Cotton and Other Plays*, and *Dragon Country*. A few titles are not discussed individually, but are subsumed in the discussions of the more important works that developed from them. These are: *Ten Blocks on the Camino Real* (see *Camino Real*), *The Long Stay Cut Short; or The Unsatisfactory Supper* (see *Baby Doll*), *Twenty-seven Wagons Full of Cotton* (see *Baby Doll*), and *Confessional* (see *Small Craft Warnings*).

# INTRODUCTION

"I am Blanche DuBois," Tennessee Williams has said on more than one occasion. He refers, of course, to the sensitive and neurotic, yet iron-willed heroine of *A Streetcar Named Desire*, a character who has clearly entered the realm of American mythology. In the PBS television documentary "Tennessee Williams' South," Williams said, with reference to race relations in the South, "You know, I always had a feeling that I am black." What Williams is saying in both instances is that he has never felt himself to be a part of the mainstream of American life; this is evident in the compassion and understanding with which he writes of the misfit, the deformed, and the damned. Williams's claim to being both white (*blanche*) and black—if those words are taken at face value—provides a metaphor for the man and his work.

Tennessee Williams is a man of striking contrasts. In a series of *New York Post* articles on Williams (April 21–25, April 27–May 4, 1958), Robert Rice observed:

He is undoubtedly one of the most trusting, sus-
spicious, generous, egocentric, helpless, self-reliant,
fearful, courageous, absentminded, observant,
modest, vain, withdrawn, gregarious, puritanical,
Bohemian, angry, mild, unsure, self-confident men
in the U.S.

The accuracy of most of Rice's observations is cor-
roborated by what Williams's friends have written
about him and, most of all, by Williams's writing on
himself. Besides his *Memoirs*, Williams has published
numerous articles of a confessional nature. He has
been perennially willing to share with the public
anecdotes of his professional achievements and frus-
trations, descriptions of his sensory responses, and
analyses of his emotional heights and depths. In short,
while he has been reluctant to discuss his own work
analytically, he has made a fetish of self-revelation.
In that regard, he wrote, in one of his many *New
York Times* articles ("Let Me Hang It All Out,"
March 4, 1973):

I have always been much concerned with the
matter of lying and I can honestly say that it is a
matter of considerable pride with me and of still
more considerable embarrassment to the publishers of my forthcoming memoirs that I simply
refuse to dissimulate the facts of my life—or of
others, I might add.

It is ironic, as well as revealing, that the most sympathetic and attractive of all of Williams's self-
portraits emerges from writing that he never intended
for publication: *Tennessee Williams' Letters to Donald Windham, 1940–1965*. In those spontaneous out-
pourings of states of mind to a friend, one may fully
appreciate the man's wit, warmth, and above all, his

generosity. Yet many of his friends have testified to the violence of his often unprovoked displays of temper. Again in the New York *Times* ("I Am Widely Regarded as the Ghost of a Writer," May 8, 1977), Williams wrote:

> But my dreams are full of alarm and wild suspicion. The world about me seems hostile. I react to unimportant defects and half-imagined slights with an indignation sometimes exploding into fury not wise in a man with vascular problems.

Not only do black-and-white contrasts exist in Williams's personality, they are evident in his written work, as well. The average American thinks of the man and his work in the same way as he once wryly characterized himself: "the one who writes all those dirty plays." Yet the underlying motive of many of his dramas is a search for purity. Whether Williams is primarily a sensation-seeker as some critics insist, or whether, as Williams says, his intention is "to illuminate the mainstream of life" with shocking material serving only to heighten the dramatic effect, he does tend to dwell on the sordid and the perverse. Yet no other American playwright has analyzed women with such subtlety and compassion. No other has come as close to creating a poetry of the theater embodied in dialogue, scenic environment, and in such theatrical devices as music, symbolic props, sound and lighting effects—all combining to create a seamless lyric impression. Despite the fact that he has written some of the most poetic lines spoken on the American stage, however, his poetry as such (two collections of poems: *In the Winter of Cities* and *Androgyne, Mon Amour*) is extremely uneven.

Like his personality, Williams's position in American theater does not fall neatly into the gray middle range. Many see him as the greatest living American playwright. At the very least, he is in company with the best dramatists this country has produced: Edward Albee, Lillian Hellman, Arthur Miller, Eugene O'Neill, Clifford Odets, Thornton Wilder. Despite that consensus, Williams has not had a new play favorably reviewed by New York theater critics in general since *The Night of the Iguana* opened on Broadway in 1961. Because of reviewers' negative response to *The Red Devil Battery Sign* in its June 1975 Boston tryout, Williams chose to have his next play open as far as possible from New York. *This Is (An Entertainment)* was staged by San Francisco's American Conservatory Theater in January 1976. Two plays, *Eccentricities of a Nightingale* and *Vieux Carré*, had New York premieres within the following year and a half, but again Williams failed to win the critics.

The harshness of reviewers in the 1960s and early 1970s did not undermine Williams's apparent confidence in his work or his will to continue his writing. He still spends, as he always has, from two to six hours a day on his writing every morning without exception. With a relatively new-discovered serenity, since the mid-1970s, he has found it in himself to excuse the critics, saying that "because of poor health, I allowed good plays, like *Kingdom of Earth*, to come in thirty minutes too long."

Williams's only lingering regret is that it has been so difficult for critics, academics, and audiences alike to allow for his evolution as a playwright away from the "poetic naturalism" of his greatest successes. His recent works seem to point in the direction of looser construction, more stylized characterization, and more open social criticism. Of course, Williams has always been interested in unconventional techniques, even as early as *The Glass Menagerie*, with its screen devices and nonrealistic lighting. And in 1976 he told San Francisco interviewer Lee Hartgrave that "there is implicit criticism of society in everything I've written from *The Glass Menagerie* to all of them." He said that he does not expect the transitions from one style to another to be treated seriously all at once, but that, since he himself has changed and the condition of the world has changed, it would be impossible for him to keep repeating the kind of work that made him popular in the 1940s and 1950s.

Like *Camino Real*, which seemed so engimatic in its 1953 Broadway premiere and quite contemporary in its revival seventeen years later, Williams's current experiments may one day prove to have been ahead of their time in anticipating new directions for American theater. Even if the general public does not fully appreciate his trailblazing efforts and fails to realize, for example, that *Out Cry* is in its own way as fine a piece of theater as *A Streetcar Named Desire*, the number and quality of Williams's undisputed "classics" should have earned him the right now to challenge himself and our expectations.

The major events of Williams's life are widely known. His own experiences have provided material for his plays from *The Glass Menagerie* to *Vieux Carré*. Book-length biographies have been written by his mother Edwina Dakin Williams, by his long-time friend Gilbert Maxwell, and by Benjamin Nelson. More useful here than a condensed biography, then, is a brief examination of some important influences on his work: his family, his Southern background, and the presence of death in his life.

Although Williams insists that all of his characters were "more or less created," it is not difficult to recognize in them the members of his family, after whom many of his characters are patterned. Of his immediate family Williams once wrote to Kenneth Tynan (the letter is published in *Tennessee Williams' Letters to Donald Windham*):

> I used to have a terrific crush on the female members of my family, mother, sister, grandmother, and hated my father, a typical pattern for homosexuals. I've stopped hating my father and I do hope you won't put in any hurtful things about him. He was not a man capable of examining his behavior toward his family, or not capable of changing it. My mother devoted herself to us three kids and developed an hostility toward him, which he took out on me, the first male to replace him. . . . He came from one of the most distinguished families in the South, being directly descended from two colonial governors and countless notable figures in southern history, but he grew up under rough circumstances after the family fortune had been entirely dissipated and without a mother. (She died soon after his birth.)

Williams's father C.C. Williams, a shoe salesman, inspired the characters of Mr. Charlie (*The Last of My Solid Gold Watches*), Big Daddy (*Cat on a Hot Tin Roof*), and the absent father in *The Glass Menagerie*. C.C.'s boisterous all-night poker games were remembered and used in the writing of *A Streetcar Named Desire*. Williams did have a more admired male role model, however, in the person of his grandfather Reverend Walter Dakin, a man of great dignity and presence, whom Williams has described along with his grandmother Dakin as "almost archetypes of 'the

gentle ones.' " Nonno in *The Night of the Iguana*
was patterned after Reverend Dakin, even down to his
preference for linen napkins rather than paper ones.

Everyone except "Miss Edwina" herself recognized
Williams's mother in the character of Amanda Wingfield (*The Glass Menagerie*). Her view on the matter
is recorded in her book *Remember Me to Tom*: "The
only resemblance that I have to Amanda is that we
both like jonquils." Gilbert Maxwell, who met Williams's mother on several occasions, has observed that
"he has written her into the character of Amanda . . .
and of Alma Winemiller in *Summer and Smoke,* cap-
turing the qualities of her personality, her wit, the
manner of her voice and gestures." In a *New York
Times* interview ("Broadway Discovers Tennessee
Williams," December 21, 1975), Robert Berkvist asked
if Miss Edwina appears in any other plays. Williams's
reply was: "In all of 'em, I guess. She had the gift of
gab. I must say she contributed a lot to my writing—
her forms of expression, for example. And that underlying hysteria gave her great eloquence. I still find
her totally mystifying—and frightening. It's best we
stay away from our mothers."

Some of Williams's most lyrical writing relates to
his unfortunate sister Rose. "My sister was quicker
at everything than I," goes the first line of his poem
"The Paper Lantern." During childhood, Williams's
lively, imaginative sister, two years older than he, was
an adored companion. They drew even closer together
when the family moved to St. Louis and the two were
bewildered by the "snobbery" of middle-class neighbors. In his short story "The Resemblance Between a
Violin-Case and a Coffin," Williams writes of his sense
of personal loss when Rose "moved before me into that
country of mysterious differences where children grow
up. . . . My sister had been magically suited to the

wild country of childhood but . . . between childhood and adulthood there is a broken terrain which is possibly even wilder than childhood was. The wilderness is interior."

Unlike Laura in *The Glass Menagerie* and "Portrait of a Girl in Glass," Rose did have dates with boys. Williams has said that Rose resembled Laura only in her vulnerability, her awareness of being "different." On a date, Williams writes in *Memoirs,* Rose would "talk with an almost hysterical animation which few young men know how to take." In this regard, one is reminded of Alma in *Summer and Smoke* and in *Eccentricities of a Nightingale*. In both plays Alma finally rebels against a rigidly sheltered upbringing by giving herself over to her physical impulses. Williams believes that this was the reason for Rose's gradual decline from eccentricity into *dementia praecox*. He writes in "Paper Lantern":

> . . . for love's explosion, defined as early
>     madness,
> consumingly shone in her transparent heart
>     for a season
> and burned it out, a tissue-paper lantern!
>     —torn from a string!
>     —tumbled across a pavilion!
> flickering three times, almost seeming to
>     cry . . .
> My sister was quicker at everything than I.

Williams was away at the University of Iowa when his parents consented to having a prefrontal lobotomy —one of the first of these dangerous and now discontinued operations in the United States—performed on Rose, leaving her peaceful but unable to cope with the world outside an institution. Ever since he became self-supporting, Williams took full financial responsi-

bility for his sister; he has provided the finest psychiatric care and established a trust fund in her name.
"This is probably the best thing I've done with my
life," he says, "besides a few bits of work." The last
line of his poem "Events Proceed" from *Androgyne,
Mon Amour* is:

> (Perhaps my life has done enough good when
>     I open
> the doors of a state asylum for my sister, if
>     only for three days
> a week, in a place called Lead Wood,
>     Missouri.)

Although Williams did not know of his parents'
decision until too late, his sense of guilt is apparent
in *The Glass Menagerie*, as is his lingering horror
twenty years after the operation, in *Suddenly Last
Summer*. Gilbert Maxwell discusses how *The Rose
Tattoo* symbolically reveals Williams's preoccupation
with his sister, and this would apply also to his poem
"A Liturgy of Roses." The last pages of *Memoirs* are
devoted entirely to Rose. Perhaps his most hauntingly
lovely tribute to her is the drama of his maturity, the
brother-sister play *Out Cry*.

Finally, there is Thomas Lanier—or Tennessee—
Williams himself. The experiences of his childhood
and youth have had tremendous influence on his
work, which is unusually subjective for one whose best
writing is in the dramatic mode, since drama requires
more artistic objectivity than other literary forms. His
two novels provide what are probably the most complex projections of his own persona into his characters.
Donald Windham refers to *The Roman Spring of
Mrs. Stone* as Williams's "first fictionalized self-
portrait after his success—and it displays a hair-raising

degree of self-knowledge." Moreover, a thirty-year-old "distinguished failed writer" from the South, an aging "derelict" playwright, and a nonconforming lady painter in *Moise and the World of Reason* are all avatars of various facets of Williams. In his *Yale/ Theatre* review of *Memoirs* (Fall 1976), Michael Lassell sees the latter novel as a "perfect 'companion piece' to the *Memoirs*," a "subtle self-portrait, as unromanticized as *Memoirs* is indulgent."

What is presented factually in his letters, essays, and interviews, and in *Memoirs*, is reconstituted artistically not only in the novels, but also in the poems, short stories, and plays. Williams has said that although his plays are not autobiographical, they do "reflect somehow the particular psychological turmoil I was going through when I wrote them" (*New York Times*, December 21, 1975). He also says that he never gave a character any emotion that he himself has not experienced. An example is the feeling expressed in Quentin's long speech in *Small Craft Warnings*: awareness of his loss of the capacity for astonishment. In the PBS-TV documentary "Tennessee Williams' South," Williams said, referring to the speech as his best piece of writing in ten years and one which justifies the entire play: "I had felt that before, but had never been able to express it in my work." But he had expressed it apart from his work some fifteen years earlier in his 1955 letter to Kenneth Tynan: "steadily life takes away from you, bit by bit, step by step, the quality of fresh involvement, new, startling reactions to experience. . . ."

Another result of his subjectiveness as a writer is the repetition of certain images and turns of phrase throughout his work. It is as if, as he says, Williams inhabits his own country ("it's where my head is, I guess"). In the plays set in the South, there are recurring references to Moon Lake, Paradise Dance Hall, Delta Planters' Hotel, and towns such as Blue Mountain and Glorious Hill, Mississippi. On a more abstract level there is Beanstalk Country, or alternatively, Dragon Country. This is probably the same madness-inducing wasteland as Tierra Incognita in *Camino Real.* One journeys alone into Beanstalk Country, as did Alexandra Del Lago of *Sweet Bird of Youth,* or into Dragon Country as did Character One in *I Can't Imagine Tomorrow.* It would seem that artists are the "jacks who climb the beanstalk country" and "tell of what they saw through cracks in the ogre's oven" ("The Beanstalk Country," from *In the Winter of Cities*). Unquestionably, Williams has made that journey.

Again borrowing from his own experience, Williams gave to Hannah Jelkes (*The Night of the Iguana*) his own "blue devils." He described the "blue devils" in himself in a letter to Donald Windham, July 28, 1947:

> My nerves are tied in knots today. I have plunged into one of my periodic neuroses, I call them "blue devils," and it is like having wild-cats under my skin. They are a Williams family trait, I suppose. Destroyed my sister's mind and made my father a raging drunkard. In me they take the form of interior storms that show remarkably little from the outside but which create a deep chasm between myself and all other people, even deeper than the relatively ordinary ones of homosexuality and being an artist. It is curious the various forms they take—someday, when I have the courage, I will sit down and face them and write them all out. Now I can only speak of the symptoms, for if I look at them too closely, I feel they would spring at me more violently. Now for instance all contact with people is like a salty

finger stroking a raw wound. . . . Ever since I was about ten years old I have lived with these blue devils of various kinds and degrees, they come and go, all of them at their crises achieving about the same intensity, none of them ever quite reaching the innermost me.

Hannah Jelkes also speaks of one of Williams's own literary heroes, Hart Crane. And, further, through the same character he reveals a preoccupation with "incomplete sentences" which is to come to full fruition in *Moise and the World of Reason*. In that novel, throughout which the incomplete sentence is used as a leitmotiv, the "distinguished failed writer"—narrator finally surmises: "I guess this aversion to completion is another serious flaw in my concept of creative work." In Williams's own case, it is the trait which compels him to remake his short stories into plays and to rewrite his plays, sometimes over a decade or so, resulting in the publication of several versions of essentially the same work.

Any thorough reader of Williams's work will note the constant reappearance of favorite images such as birds, cats, foxes, fox-teeth in the heart and in the gut, Don Quixote, a lamp or a candle at night, ice and snow, gauzy summer gowns, Arthur Rimbaud and his drunken boat, stairways and narrow passages, partitions and doors between people, ceremonial tea drinking, scavenging for food, and devices marking the passage of time. His themes, which will be discussed in relation to specific plays, include: fear (of loneliness, of loss, of death), search for a lost ideal (youth, purity, involvement), honesty vs. mendacity, the need for compassion and tenderness among all people isolated in their separate skins. His compassion focuses most frequently on the elderly and the lonely, on women, artists, blacks, and helpless sensualists, and on any derelict whose luck has run out but who attempts to salvage a bit of dignity.

Tennessee Williams is a Southern American writer. His childhood was spent in the South, and his long exposure to Southern speech patterns is largely responsible for the musicality of his dialogue, a characteristic which he calls "hysterical eloquence." Of his style, he said (in *Theatre Arts,* January 1962):

> My great bête noir as a writer has been a tendency to what people call . . . to poeticize, you know, and that's why I suppose I've written so many Southern heroines. They have a tendency to gild the lily, and they speak in a rather florid style which seems to suit me because I write out of emotion, and I get carried away by the emotion.

Their reliance on charm is another characteristic of Southern women which attracts Williams to write about them. That eloquence and charm may be glimpsed in his mother Edwina Dakin Williams when she writes in *Remember Me to Tom* a sentence such as the following: "Southern men seem a little embarrassed to let their wives work, and therefore, the women have more time to spend taking care of the house and themselves. No matter how difficult the drudgery all day, I always took a bath in the evening and changed to a dainty dress for dinner, as did Rose."

What Williams loves about the South itself is its "greater sense of honor, of decency," that is, the Southern qualities of courage and gallantry which he wrote into such characters as Amanda Wingfield and even the little girl in *This Property Is Condemned.* In comparison with the North, he feels that there is "less of a dog-eat-dog attitude" and less intense pressure on people to conform. He often depicts Southern society as characterized by an attitude of romantic melancholy or by a kind of aristocratic decay, very like the Russian milieux of his favorite author Chekhov. At the same time he acknowledged his own rebellion against a puritanical repressiveness in the Bible Belt mentality.

He is disturbed, too, by the South's conservatism in its social point of view. One example of this concern expressed through his work is in *Kingdom of Earth*. After seducing Myrtle, Chicken tells her that he may be as much as one-quarter Negro. Williams notes Myrtle's reaction as "the typical Southern lower-class dread and awe of Negroes." Chicken goes on to explain how his dark complexion has forced him to live "the life of a dawg that nobody owns and owns nothing." And by contrasting Chicken with his fair-haired half-brother Lot, who is ultimately perceived as a malevolent, almost satirical version of Blanche DuBois, Williams suggests what he meant by always having had "a feeling I am black." Yet, if Williams finds prejudices, perversions, and neuroses among Southerners, it must not be seen as a betrayal of the country of his heart. "If I were writing about Yankees, I promise you, I would find every bit as much 'damnation' among them—and not as much charm," he said, as quoted by his mother in *Remember Me to Tom*. And in the PBS program "Tennessee Williams' South," he added, "I can't expect all Southerners to realize that writing about them is an act of love, but it is."

The charm of Southern expression surfaces even when Williams speaks of death, a subject which has long been one of his major obsessions. In *Memoirs* he wrote:

> Death is the unavoidable eventuality which in most cases we avoid as long as we can, but which, finally, when all the possible options have expired, we must attempt to accept with as much grace as there remains in our command.

It was in the spring of 1946 that the "shadow of death" began to hang heavily over his life and work. The incident is recounted in *Memoirs*, in his 1955 letter to Kenneth Tynan, and in a letter to Donald Windham from the hospital at the time. He was driving alone from St. Louis to Taos, New Mexico when both he and his car broke down in Alva, Oklahoma. A local doctor wrongly diagnosed his severe, stabbing pains as appendicitis and sent him to a hospital in Wichita. He was kept there three days for observation, then was told he probably had a chronically irritated appendix, and was released. Williams went on to Taos, where a medically rare *maecles diverticulum* operation in the small hospital there saved his life. For three years afterward, he lived with a premonition of imminent death, but he feels that the experience produced some of his best work, particularly *Cat on a Hot Tin Roof*, in which he was able to come to grips directly with the subject of death.

A second period of especially intense awareness of death—even, apparently, of a chronic death wish—lasted approximately from 1963 to 1969, the years he calls his "Stoned Age." It was at the beginning of that period that he wrote *The Milk Train Doesn't Stop Here Anymore*, his most protracted dramatic dissertation on the subject of death. To Williams, death is oblivion, and the only way to cheat oblivion is to leave a body of artistic work behind. He believes that writers are obsessed with death because they must undergo two deaths—their own and that of their creative flow. Thus, he agreed to write *Memoirs* because he thought he would be dead before it was published. While his art now enjoys a resurgence of grass-roots popularity, the fact that his life, too, has moved out of the psychological shadow of death may be seen in his recent statement to *Washington Star* interviewer David Richards: "Once upon a time I thought of calling my memoirs 'Flee, Flee This Sad Hotel' which is a line from a poem by Anne Sexton who did kill herself, but then that's really quite false. I don't really regard my life as a sad hotel any more than a merry tavern. I certainly don't intend to vacate it until I'm kicked out."

# I. EARLY ONE-ACT PLAYS:
*Staking Out the Territory*

## *1. At Liberty*

All of the major books about Williams neglect to mention *At Liberty*, a one-act play which does not appear in any anthology of Williams's plays. However, unlike so many others of his early plays—*Cairo! Shanghai! Bombay!*, *The Magic Tower, Headlines, Me, Vashya!*, *The Fugitive Kind*, *Candles to the Sun, Spring Storm, Not About Nightingales,* and *Stairs to the Roof*—this one has been published. It is included, with *This Property Is Condemned*, under the joint heading "Landscape with Figures; Two Mississippi Plays," in William Kozlenko's *American Scenes* (1941), and it appears again in Betty Smith's *25 Non-Royalty One-Act Plays for All-Girl Casts* (1942).

There are two characters in *At Liberty*: Gloria Bessie Greene (stage name, Gloria La Greene) and her mother, who functions as a dramatic foil to Gloria. The play is set in their tasteless living room in a small Mississippi town. It is two-thirty in the morning when Gloria returns from an evening with a "picked-up acquaintance" she met at the Delta Planters' Hotel.

Gloria, a "thin feverish-looking blonde whose stage

experience is stated with undue emphasis in her make-up," is one of several predecessors of Blanche DuBois to appear in the one-act plays. Her plight illustrates a theme that Williams has used repeatedly: that of the artist or dreamer in confinement. Gloria was once a dancer in road shows, but is now back home in Blue Mountain, Mississippi, with a chronic chest ailment.

At age thirty-two, she still has the option, her mother reminds her, of marrying a small-town boy who has long held open for her the offer of a home and respectability. But that choice would be to Gloria, like the enforced rest-recovery period in Blue Mountain, a kind of living death. She chooses instead to court early death by indulging her passion for life—running around at night with strangers, while hoping for results from an ad she placed in *Billboard* magazine. The ad announced that Gloria La Greene is "at liberty" for casting in stage productions. Valiant, eternally optimistic little trouper though she is, Gloria breaks down at the end of the play when she realizes the full irony of the term "at liberty."

## 2. *Moony's Kid Don't Cry*

*Moony's Kid Don't Cry* is a variation on the theme used in *At Liberty*, which has, in fact, continued to interest Williams for more than twenty-five years—the theme of the dreamer-poet in confinement. In *Moony's Kid Don't Cry* and in several plays and stories Williams wrote in the 1940s, a sensitive soul is caught in the numbing grind of life in a big industrial city, while in later plays—*Out Cry*, for example—the confinement is spiritual. Moony is a hulking young lumberjack-turned-factory-worker, outwardly not unlike Stanley Kowalski. But, inarticulate though he may be, Moony's romantic yearnings relate him closely to Tom in *The Glass Menagerie*.

The action occurs in the squalid kitchen of a city flat; the season is indicated by a dime-store Christmas tree on the kitchen table. There is also a washline with diapers and an incongruously splendid hobbyhorse. Moony's wife, Jane, a frail, sickly creature in a shabby kimono, reproaches Moony for his extravagance in buying the hobbyhorse for their month-old baby. Moony speaks nostalgically of the North Woods, the St. Lawrence River, and of the night ten months ago that he met Jane at the Paradise dance-hall, when he let his desire outweigh his need for freedom. Jane's response is to natter about the baby's bowel movements and the gifts and propositions she had had from her boss before marriage to Moony. He speaks of giving up his factory job and chopping "a way through this world" for the family, although even the artificial Christmas tree seems to stand in contradiction to the power of his axe. Angered by Jane's mockery of his "crazy" idea, Moony throws her against the wall and prepares to walk out on her. Jane staggers to her feet and stops him, saying: "There's something you got to take with you! Your property, Moony—you might as well take it along!" She brings him the baby, then runs out of the room. Moony's escape takes a new route as he becomes absorbed in showing off the hobby-horse to his infant son.

On April 16, 1958, *Moony's Kid Don't Cry* was shown on NBC-TVs "Kraft Theatre," along with *This Property Is Condemned* and *The Last of My Solid Gold Watches*.

## 3. The Dark Room

The Dark Room is the least successful piece of dramatic writing in *American Blues*. The characters are flat, and the ending falls short of its intended shock effect. In the stage directions, Williams himself describes Miss Morgan, a spinsterish social worker, as "pretty much a stock character." She interviews Mrs. Pocciotti, a ponderous "avalanche of female flesh" with smoldering, suspicious eyes. Through the Italian woman's curt half-answers, we piece together a murky portrait of her daughter who, six months before, had shut herself away in a dark room. This series of discoveries—revelations about the past which throw light on the present situation—constitutes the entire dramatic action of the play. *The Dark Room* adumbrates a masterful use of the same pattern in *Suddenly Last Summer*, but here, the final revelation does not bring about a reversal of circumstances like the one which allows the later, longer play to approach the magnitude of Greek tragedy.

## 4. The Case of the Crushed Petunias

Although the plays in *American Blues* might be described as juvenilia, *The Case of the Crushed Petunias* is set apart by its fanciful, *faux-naïf* quality and gentle humor. The protagonist is a pretty, twenty-six-year-old spinster in the town of Primanproper, near Boston. She has "barricaded her house and her heart behind a double row of petunias."

As the play opens, Miss Dorothy Simple complains to a police officer that during the night someone with a size eleven-D foot has methodically trampled all of her petunias. The next visitor to her Simple Notion Shop is a Young Man who admits to having size eleven-D feet. He crushed her petunias because they represented an overly dainty, inflexible, everything-in-its-place mentality. He offers to replace her petunias with wild roses. He also offers to show her the wonder and variety and excitement of life that is "not behind petunias," if only she will meet him that night at half-past eight on Highway No. 77, "by the wild plum tree—at the broken place in the long stone wall—where roots have cleft the rocks and made them crumble." A newly awakened romantic impulse in her responds to his imagery, and she agrees. Simple Notions are abandoned in favor of Tremendous Inspirations. Dorothy Simple becomes what Williams once called himself—a rebellious puritan.

## 5. The Purification

When Williams is asked to name his favorite writers or the writers who have most influenced his own style, he invariably names Hart Crane, D.H. Lawrence, and Anton Chekhov. Occasionally he adds Rainer Maria Rilke and Federico García Lorca. The influence of Spanish poet-dramatist Lorca, whether conscious or not, seems apparent in Williams's only play in verse, *The Purification*. It is the play least typical of Williams's recognized "style."

The imagery used in *The Purification* is the same as that used in Lorca's poetic tragedies of the early 1930s: water, moon, earth, blood, the horse as a symbol of masculinity. In both cases, the characters live by a strong code of honor, and their drama is resolved by violence.

*The Purification* is set in western ranchlands similar to the country around Taos, New Mexico. The scene is a stark, white-walled, improvised courtroom. The characters are of Spanish descent, some pure Castilian, others part Indian. In Lorca's *Blood Wedding*, all but one of the characters are given generic rather than individual names, and Williams employs the same device, designating his major characters as the Judge, the Son, the Mother, the Father, the Rancher from Casa Rojo. He uses a Chorus of Ranchers to echo and intensify moments in the dialogue; one is reminded of the chorus in Lorca's *Yerma*. In addition, some of Williams's blank verse could almost be mistaken for a translation of Lorca. These lines from Scene 1 are a striking example:

> You, Mother, would wash
> the delicate white lace curtains,
> sweep down the long stairs
> and scent the alcoves with lemon.

In *The Purification*, two crimes are recounted. The Son of the family from Casa Blanca had carried on an incestuous affair with his sister, who was married unwillingly to the Rancher from Casa Rojo. One morning at daybreak, the Rancher crept up where the brother and sister were lying together and killed the girl with an axe.

The trial is interrupted twice, by two different apparitions of the dead girl. The Son sees her as Elena of the Springs, wearing a sheer white robe, looking cool and crystalline. Later, the Rancher sees her as Elena of the Desert, "the loveless bride, the water sealed under rock from the lover's thirst," in a coarse-fibred, tight-fitting garment. When the Son's vision of Elena reappears, he stumbles toward her, whips out a knife, and plunges it into his own breast, saying, "Witness—in this thrust—our purification!" The Rancher then stabs himself to cleanse his own honor. Finally, rain begins to fall on the parched land.

*The Purification* was not produced professionally until May 1954, over a decade after it was written. Margo Jones directed it on a bill with Jean Giraudoux's *The Apollo of Bellac* at her Theatre 54 in Dallas. According to Brooks Atkinson (*New York Times*, May 29, 1954), the play was "staged as if it were a religious ritual by Margo Jones in her best form and it is acted with grace and devoutness by a company inspired by what they are playing."

## 6. The Lady of Larkspur Lotion

In terms of dramatic structure, *The Lady of Larkspur Lotion* is merely a build-up to a punchline, and the punchline is an amusing tribute to another of Williams's favorite authors. But it is the quick-sketch portraits of the characters and the poignancy of their brave, romantic fantasies against a squalid backdrop that have made this very short play one of Williams's most popular.

Mrs. Hardwicke-Moore, a dyed-blonde woman of forty, living in a cockroach-infested, rented room in the French Quarter of New Orleans, may be seen as an early incarnation of Blanche DuBois. Her manner is affected, and she takes refuge from reality by pretending to be the owner of a Brazilian rubber plantation. On her dresser, however, is a bottle of Larkspur Lotion, a common treatment for body vermin; this suggests that she has been supporting herself by prostitution.

The other two characters are Mrs. Wire and the

Writer. Both will reappear some twenty-five years
later, their names and basic drives unchanged, in
*Vieux Carré*. Mrs. Wire, the hard-bitten landlady, is
not taken in by Mrs. Hardwicke-Moore's tale of a forthcoming delayed quarterly dividend from the rubber
plantation. She demands payment of the rent and
humiliates her roomer with the mock title "The Lady
of Larkspur Lotion."

Williams has an unerring sense of when to add
humor to pathos. One such example is when the
Writer bursts into the room and, in a fit of drunken
chivalry, cries, "Stop persecuting this woman!" He
defends Mrs. Hardwicke-Moore's right "to compensate
for the cruel deficiencies of reality by the exercise of
a little—what shall I say?—God-given—imagination."
Mrs. Wire now directs her venom toward the Writer
and his supposed "780-page masterpiece." She exits,
delivering an ultimatum: "Tomorrow morning!
money or out you go! Both of you! Both together!
780-page masterpiece and Brazilian rubber plantation!
BALONEY!"

The two derelicts face each other. The Writer
questions the Lady about her plantation in Brazil and
gently encourages her to describe its view of the Medi-
terranean and of the White Cliffs of Dover. Then,
when she asks his name, he replies, "Chekhov! Anton
Pavlovitch Chekhov!"

## 7. *The Last of My Solid Gold Watches*

It is not coincidence that Mr. Charlie Colton,
the protagonist of *The Last of My Solid Gold
Watches*, has the same initials as Williams's father.
The play is a portrait of a traveling shoe salesman
who, at seventy-eight, is still "going strong," but has

outlived his era. It is virtually a monologue spoken by the "old war-horse" to two other characters in turn: an old Negro hotel porter and a vapid young salesman. Mr. Charlie is loquacious, egotistical, and hot-tempered, but he also reveals himself to be a man of integrity. Of his own salesman father, Williams wrote in his *Memoirs*: "A catalogue of the unattractive aspects of his personality would be fairly extensive, but towering above them were, I think, two great virtues which I hope are hereditary: total honesty and total truth, as he saw it, in his dealings with others."

The torn window blinds and the broken ceiling fan in a hotel room often occupied by Mr. Charlie during his forty-six years on the road testify to the theme of the play: decline and deterioration. Mr. Charlie muses aloud on the recent deaths of three other old-timers. He blusters about the modern world's loss of concern for quality, both in commercial products and in human relations. He shows off the fifteen solid gold watches he had been awarded as ranking salesman of the year for his shoe company, and he realizes that he has already received "the last" of his solid gold watches.

One can scarcely refrain from comparing this short play to Arthur Miller's full-length *Death of a Salesman*, which appeared in 1949, two years after the first production of *The Last of My Solid Gold Watches*. Both plays depict once-successful salesmen who can no longer keep up with youthful competitors and technological progress. The essential distinction is that Miller's Willy Loman had always relied on exactly the shallow qualities that Charlie Colton deplores —style, smartness, outward appearances. Willy Loman has no set of solid values and he finally is a defeated man, driven to suicide. Mr. Charlie, in contrast, may know by his watches that his time is just about over, but his faith in tradition, his pride in the quality of the product he sells, and his sense of personal dignity will never run down.

## 8. Portrait of a Madonna

The values professed by Miss Lucretia Collins in *Portrait of a Madonna* are those of genteel Southern womanhood nurtured by the Episcopal church. She now lives in a northern city, where her ill-kept apartment living room is an appropriate setting for her disordered ramblings, which combine memory and fantasy.

An understanding apartment manager, a protective elderly porter, and a cynical elevator boy listen to the breathless chatter of this prim spinster with girlish curls and ribbons, who insists that she has been visited repeatedly by a man who breaks into her bedroom and "indulges his senses." Her frustration and guilt feelings, thinly masked by religious scruples and social hypocrisies, surface as she tells her story. Thirty years before, she had loved a fellow Sunday-school teacher and lost him to a shameless girl from Cincinnati who disappeared with him from a picnic and returned with grass stains on the seat of her skirt. Miss Collins had fled the Southern town where she would have been doomed to walk home from church every week, under a brutal sun, past the house where Richard had installed his bride, and where his six children were born. And now, after all these years, it was he who had found her and made nightly visits to her bedroom.

Three times in the course of the play Miss Collins tells her visitors that: "Mother will bring in something cool after while." The others know that her mother has been dead for fifteen years and is no more likely to materialize than the baby Miss Collins announces she is going to have. She plans to give the child a private education "where it won't come under the evil influence of the Christian church!" She doesn't want it to "grow up in the shadow of the cross and then have to walk along blocks that scorch you with terrible sunlight." This visionary portrait of herself as a madonna reveals her deep dissatifaction with a religion that makes no allowance for sensual fulfillment, and with a social definition—that of a Southern lady—that fails to prepare her to cope with life.

Miss Collins's girlhood, with its unattainable love object, has much in common with that of Alma Winemiller in *Summer and Smoke*. In the final sequence, which foreshadows Blanche's departure at the end of *A Streetcar Named Desire*, a Doctor and Nurse lead Miss Collins off to the asylum.

## 9. *Auto-Da-Fé*

The play's title is a term borrowed from the Spanish Inquisition; it literally means "act of faith" and refers to the burning of a heretic. The heresy of Eloi, a young man in his thirties, is gradually revealed as he chats with his domineering mother on the porch of their decaying boarding house in the Vieux Carré of New Orleans. They discuss the corruption and degeneracy of their neighborhood, which Eloi believes should be condemned and purified by fire. He turns the conversation to himself, hinting at his own need for purification.

Eloi is obsessed with a lewd photograph that has come into his possession. His mother's inquisition concerning it culminates in orders to burn the picture immediately, but he cannot bring himself to touch the lighted match to the picture. Instead, he rushes into the house and locks the door. There is a muffled explosion and a sudden burst of fiery light from the interior.

## 10. Lord Byron's Love Letter

The decadent milieu of *Auto-Da-Fé* was underscored by the sound of distant jukeboxes, laughter from the bars, and the street cries of a tamale vendor. The sounds of New Orleans again provide atmospheric background in *Lord Byron's Love Letter*, this time in contrast to the stage setting. It is Mardi Gras time, and the vulgar, mindless carnival noises intrude upon the closed, genteel world of a Spinster and an Old Woman in their rose-shaded parlor.

A Milwaukee Matron enters, her drunken Husband in tow. She had noticed the sign on the door and was curious about the love letter from Lord Byron. The Spinster reads portions of her grandmother's diary which describes the latter's romantic chance meeting with Lord Byron on the Acropolis when she was a girl of sixteen. Prompted by hoarse commands from the Old Woman, who has concealed herself behind the curtains, the Spinster shows the love letter and explains how, not long after it arrived, her grandmother had learned of Lord Byron's death and had gone into seclusion for the rest of her life.

The sound of the parade band grows louder on the street outside. The two tourists lurch away, ignoring the Spinster's plea for some remuneration for the display of the letter. The Old Woman cries out: "Ariadne, my letter! You've dropped my letter! Your Grandfather's letter is lying on the floor!"

The punch line of this play does not take its audience altogether by surprise. More important even than the revelation of the Old Woman's affair with Lord Byron is the sudden vividness of the contrast between the romantically idealized image of her past and the wasted, grasping creature of the present.

## *11. The Strangest Kind of Romance*

Although *The Strangest Kind of Romance* is not as richly textured or structurally cohesive a work as "The Malediction," the short story on which it is based, this "lyric play in four scenes" abounds with symbols and metaphors. The scenic metaphor is a furnished room, the walls of which are covered with signatures of the countless single working-men who have occupied it for a time. One window frames the smokestacks of a huge factory: their belching and pulsing serves as a running commentary on the action in the room. The other window shows tree branches, which indicate the passage of time, from autumn to spring, during the four scenes.

A lonely, nervous Little Man rents the room from a buxom Landlady. He adopts the cat, Nitchevo, who had belonged to the previous occupant, a Russian. The Little Man, like the Russian before him, becomes the Landlady's lover, but finds warmth of affection and understanding only with the cat who, in keeping with her name, asks "nothing" of the Little Man. His term of occupancy of the room is similar to a passage through life, with its sufferings temporarily obliterated by carnal satisfaction, but with spiritual solace gained through a "strange kind of romance" with another lost being, a cat.

An Old Man appears periodically, collecting empty bottles to trade in at the Bright Spot Delicatessen. The religious imagery in his lines and in the fact that, though blind, he seems to have extrasensory "sight" suggest that he represents God, collecting souls to take to heaven. It is he who pronounces the malediction on the factory owners who have fired the Little Man and others from their jobs. At the end of the play the Old Man accompanies the Little Man, now ghostlike after an illness, along with Nitchevo, to an unknown destination, while the light coming through the window turns more and more golden.

## 12. The Long Goodbye

The Long Goodbye is a memory play, an exploration of the technique that is more fully developed in The Glass Menagerie. Joe, a struggling writer, relives moments from the past as he watches four moving men clear the apartment he had shared with his mother and sister. The flashback sequences are perhaps Joe's way of freeing himself from an uneasy feeling of responsibility for his mother, now dead, and his sister, now leading a faintly disreputable life in another city. He recognizes that each of them had achieved her own kind of liberation. As Joe casts a departing glance about the emptied room, he hears the shouts of children playing in the street: "Olly-olly-oxen-free!"

The Long Goodbye also recalls Thornton Wilder's one-act play The Long Christmas Dinner (1931). Both plays give a sense of interwoven lives and deaths and of the possibility of beginning anew. Joe sums up an underlying premise of both plays: "You're saying goodbye all the time, every minute you live. Because that's what life is, just a long, long goodbye!"

## 13. Hello from Bertha

*The Long Goodbye* heralds a new beginning for Joe, just as, paradoxically, *Hello from Bertha* marks an ending for its title character. Bertha is a "large blonde prostitute" who has been lying sick in an alcoholic haze, earning no money for two weeks. The other girls need her room and threaten to send her off in an ambulance, but Bertha defends herself by screaming accusations of theft at them. They urge her to write to Charlie, the man she talks so much about, who runs the "biggest hardware store in Memphis." She recalls the "good times together in the back room" with Charlie, when she worked in the store, until Charlie married a little choir-singer. She tries to write and ask him for help, but all she can bring herself to say to him is "Hello from Bertha."

Williams makes a point of describing in detail the tawdriness of the setting, and he emphasizes Bertha's coarseness. The play exemplifies one of the outstanding features of Williams's early work: his ability to evoke a moment of compassion for life's most hopeless castaways.

## 14. This Property Is Condemned

*This Property Is Condemned* is a delicate tone-poem for the stage. All of the elements—characters, setting, dialogue, colors, props, and sounds—are skillfully orchestrated to create a hauntingly lyrical effect of decadence.

Willie is a child-woman of about thirteen. She carries a beat-up doll, but wears lipstick, rouge, and rhinestones. While walking tightrope-style on a railroad track, she meets a slightly older boy and imperturbably exposes her situation—abandoned by both mother and father, she is living on a legacy of fantasies inherited from her adored older sister Alva, who died of a lung infection. Willie is now the sole occupant of the boarded-up house, which had been the scene of so many parties for railroad men when Alva was alive, and is now condemned.

Adding their comment to Willie's story are a distant train whistle and crows that make "a sound of roughly torn cloth." The milky whiteness of the sky above the flat landscape continually draws Willie's notice. "White as a clean piece of paper," she says four times in the short script. She would like to draw pictures on it, and her pictures are all dreams of reliving Alva's life. The blankness of the sky reflects the loneliness Willie refuses to admit. Ironically, her soul is no longer that of a child, no longer a clean piece of paper. She exits along the track, singing Alva's favorite song, "My Blue Heaven."

A 1966 film version of the same title was "suggested" by Williams's play. In the film, Willie and the railroad-track setting are used to frame an extended story of Alva and her railroad men. Despite an outstanding cast—Natalie Wood, Robert Redford, Kate Reid, and Charles Bronson, the film was a critical failure.

## 15. Talk to Me Like the Rain and Let Me Listen . . .

Another fragile mood piece is *Talk to Me Like the Rain and Let Me Listen . . . .* A Man and a Woman occupy a furnished room with a rumpled bed.

A single open window frames a rainy sky. The whole texture of the play's imagery is based on water. The Woman sips from a tumbler of water; she has had nothing but water for an indeterminate length of time. The Man had ended his drunken outing of the night before in a bathtub full of melting ice cubes. The rain outside the window steadily increases and grows colder. The rain is the only thing that suggests the passage of time for the couple.

The Man rambles incoherently about his past and how he has been "passed around like a dirty postcard in this city." The Woman talks of the future she would like to have—fifty years of listening to the rain in lonely, uncomplicated anonymity, gradually growing pale and thin enough to be carried away by the "cool white arms of the wind." But both are rooted hopelessly in an unchanging present. Instead of making the escape she dreams about, the Woman calls the Man back to bed.

## 16. Something Unspoken

Another relationship frozen in time is that of Miss Cornelia Scott, a wealthy Southern spinster, and Grace Lancaster, Miss Scott's personal secretary. The "something unspoken" of the title remains unspoken during the conversation they have on the fifteenth anniversary of Grace's coming to live in Miss Scott's house. Their relationship continues, unaltered.

The play's most intriguing aspect is that it permits radically different interpretations of what is left unspoken—ranging from repressed desire for a lesbian relationship to seething hatred between the two ladies. The ambiguities of a love-hate relationship between two women are further explored in Williams's short story "Happy August the Tenth" in *Eight Mortal Ladies Possessed*.

*Something Unspoken* was performed in New York, off-Broadway, on a double bill with *Suddenly Last Summer*, under the joint title *Garden District*, in January 1958. Although for most critics the former was overshadowed by the latter, the review in *Theatre Arts* (March 1958) gave preference to *Something Unspoken* as "an allusive, evanescent and unpretentious little theatrical come-on that served to raise both the curtain and our hopes."

# II. FULL-LENGTH PLAYS:
*Creating a New Eden*

## *17. Battle of Angels* and *Orpheus Descending*

The dramatic statement that has been meta-morphosed under various titles—*Something Wild in the Country* (early working title), *Battle of Angels* (1940 play), *Orpheus Descending* (1957 play), and *The Fugitive Kind* (1960 film version)—is one that is close to Tennessee Williams's heart. From the aborted Theater Guild production of *Battle of Angels* to the sixty-eight performance Broadway run of *Orpheus Descending*, a period of seventeen years, Williams says he "never quit working on this one. . . . It never went into the trunk, it always stayed on the work-bench."

In his article "Tennessee Williams' Fugitive Kind" (*Modern Drama*, May 1972), Donald P. Costello points out that *Orpheus Descending* is a compendium of all of Williams's favorite images, thematic concerns, and dramatic devices. Fire and water, which alternate as metaphors for purification in the one-act plays, are here intertwined. The bird imagery that is prevalent in so many of the full-length plays takes its place here, along with such significant objects as a guitar, revolver,

snakeskin jacket, gold ring, blossoming orchard, graveyard, knives, and the sounds of train whistles and
barking dogs. Contrasts are set up not only between
shadow and light, blindness and "visions," cancer and
pregnancy, merchandising and loving or creating, but
also between the hypocritical corruption of the townspeople and the childlike qualities in the four characters with "fugitive" souls, the innocent misfits in the
town—Val, Vee, Lady, and Carol. The two versions
of the play employ an uneasy syncretism of symbols
from both Christian Scripture and Greek mythology.
It has been suggested that this overloading of the
plays may be a reason for their relative lack of success
in production. Since the later version, *Orpheus Descending*, is the more tightly constructed play and is
the one in which Williams believes he has "finally
managed to say" what he "wanted to say," it is the
one summarized here.

The setting is the interior of Torrance Mercantile
Store in a small town in Two River County, Mississippi. There are stairs to the Torrances' living quarters
on the  floor above, a small curtained-off alcove, and
an archway through which may be glimpsed a portion
of the adjoining "confectionery." The play's action
occurs during the rainy season—late winter and early
spring.

In the Prologue, Dolly and Beulah, tastelessly
dressed middle-aged housewives, set up tables in the
store and gossip about the owners, Jabe and Lady
Torrance. The two husbands go to meet the train
from Memphis, on which Lady is bringing her husband home after his operation for cancer. Beulah de-
livers a monologue, which is frankly expository, directly to the audience. She tells of Lady's father, an
Italian, who planted an orchard and opened a wine
garden, where young couples used to go courting dur-

ing Prohibition. Lady was eighteen then, and she was courted by David Cutrere, handsome scion of the county's most distinguished plantation family, but he jilted her to marry a society girl. Lady, soon afterwards, married Jabe Torrance, never knowing that he was the leader of a redneck gang from town that burned down the orchard and wine garden with her father in it, because the Italian had "sold liquor to niggers."

Scene 1 begins with the entrance of Carol Cutrere, a fragile-looking young woman in her thirties, with a childlike voice. She is on her way out of town, having been given an allowance by her brother David and his wife on condition that she stay away from Two River County. She carries a revolver and a pint of bourbon. A Negro Conjure Man enters and offers Carol a talisman, the breastbone of a bird. She tells him that it is not yet clean, that it is a black charm; it will become a white charm if it is left out "in the rain and the sun till every sign of corruption is burned and washed away from it." She asks the Conjure Man to give the Choctaw cry, and just as the wild sound ends, Val Xavier enters, wearing a snakeskin jacket and carrying a guitar. Vee Talbott, the sheriff's wife, has brought him there with the idea that Lady might hire him to help in the store now that Jabe cannot work. Val had been taken in by Vee when his car broke down in the rain the night before. It is appropriate that these two characters enter together, since his name Valentine Xavier (pronounced "Savior") suggests "love" and "Christ," and he is a musician. The charitable Vee is also an artist; she paints religious pictures from "visions," and, twice in the play, she experiences temporary blindness.

Carol is drawn to Val and tries to persuade him to join her in driving around, drinking, dancing, and possibly lovemaking on a blanket in the cemetery. Val tells her that it is his thirtieth birthday and he is finished with that kind of life. When the sickly look- ing Jabe Torrance arrives, Dolly and Beulah, their husbands Dog and PeeWee, and the spinster Temple sisters voice a chorus of flattering remarks to him. Jabe is taken directly upstairs to his bed. Then the women comment behind his back that "he has th' death sweat on him." Their venomous gossip is next directed against Carol, who has been telling Val how she first acquired her bad reputation in the town by spending her inheritance on projects to benefit the black popu- lation. She flees the hissing chorus of women. Val follows her out.

Several hours later, Val enters the now-deserted, darkened store. Lady descends the stairs and is sur- prised by him. He asks her for a job. When she ques- tions him about his background, he says that his guitar "washes me clean like water when anything unclean has touched me." He tells her about a kind of legless, transparent-winged, sky-colored bird. Those birds live their whole lives on the wing and sleep on the wind, never touching earth until they die. Lady longs to be such a bird, to escape the existence into which she sold herself when she married Jabe. She shows Val the confectionery that is being redecorated to resemble her father's orchard. She hires him to work in the store.

Act 2 takes place several weeks later. Lady has been finding fault with Val. He prepares to leave. She apologizes, saying she has not been able to sleep lately and she has not had time to get to know him. Val replies: "Nobody ever gets to know *nobody*! We're all of us sentenced to solitary confinement inside our own skins for life!" He tells how in his youth he went looking for answers, but only succeeded in becoming corrupted.

Their conversation is interrupted by a commotion signaling Carol Cutrere's arrival in town. One of the townswomen telephones from the store for David Cutrere to come and get his sister. Carol enters and asks to speak privately with Val. She begs him to come away with her, because she has had a presentiment of danger for him if he remains there. David comes for Carol, and although Lady has forbidden him to enter the store, she now impulsively calls him back. In their moment alone together, she tells him that she was going to have his baby the summer he quit her, but she "had it cut out of my body, and they cut my heart out with it!" That had enabled her to sell herself to Jabe and his store, just as David sold himself in marriage to wealth. As Jabe pounds his cane on the floor above to summon Lady, she and David reveal the anguish each still feels. David exits, Val reenters, and Lady moans, "I made a fool of myself!"

A brief scene of mutual understanding between Val and Vee bridges the time Lady is upstairs giving Jabe his morphine. Val starts to leave for the night, but Lady asks him to stay and talk. They hear the distant baying of chain-gang dogs chasing some runaway convict. A shot is fired and the baying dies out. Lady offers to let Val move into the curtained alcove in the store. He hesitates, but she insists and goes upstairs to get linens for the bed. While she is off stage, Val takes his guitar and some money from the cashbox, and he leaves.

Late that night Val enters in the dark and replaces money in the cashbox from a larger wad. Discovering him by flashlight, Lady accuses him of stealing. He explains that he borrowed less than she owes him and used it to win at blackjack, enough to quit his job the next day and move on. If she is disappointed in him, he is with her also for going after him in the same way as have so many women. Val starts for the door, but Lady intercepts him and cries: "No, no, don't go. . . . I need you!!! To live. . . . To go on living!!!" Val goes into the alcove, and Lady follows him.

In Act 3 it is the Saturday before Easter, the date set for the gala opening of the Torrance Confectionery. Early in the morning, Lady runs downstairs to warn Val to get dressed, because Jabe is coming downstairs and does not know that Val sleeps there. Jabe, supported by his hired nurse, looks over Val and the confectionery. With its artificial branches of fruit trees in flower and soft lights in white arbors, the confectionery reminds Jabe of when he helped burn down "the Wop's" wine garden. Lady is overcome upon learning of Jabe's part in the cause of her father's death.

Just at sunset, with brilliant light breaking through the rain clouds, Vee Talbott gropes her way into the store. She says she had been struck blind. This repeats the pattern of her previous scene with Val, which also occurred during a fiery sunset. Vee has just had a vision of the eyes of Christ, eyes so bright that they burned out her own eyes. Val places a compress on her eyes, but his touch brings a violent reaction. She looks into his eyes as though seeing her vision of Christ again, falls to her knees, and clasps her arms about Val. Sheriff Talbott enters to discover Val, for the second time, with his hands on Mrs. Talbott. Vee is roughly taken outside. The sheriff, Dog, and PeeWee pull knives on Val and threaten to break his guitar. Sheriff Talbott orders Val out of the county by sunrise.

The final scene occurs half an hour later. It is already dark; passers-by outside the store resemble "shades in the under kingdom." The distant hounds bay restlessly. The chorus of gossiping women discusses Jabe's hemorrhage and the fact that Lady has been away from him all day, still preparing to open the confectionery for the after-movie crowd that night. Carol arrives, looking for Val to drive her across the river, since her license has been revoked. She asks the Conjure Man to give the Choctaw cry. Val enters on cue, while the "chorus" is frightened away. When Lady and Val are alone, she tells him to put on his white waiter's jacket. She is determined to bring the wine garden to life while Jabe is still alive, as this will be her triumph over him. Val puts on the snakeskin jacket. He tells Lady he would have left before she got back to the store, but he wanted to tell her that he loves her and will wait for her outside Two River County. She pleads with him to stay just until Jabe dies, but he remains firm. Jabe's nurse comes downstairs on her way out for a dinner break. Lady and the nurse quarrel, a sequence which builds up to Lady's admission that she is pregnant. The nurse exits, determined to tell the whole town. Now Lady realizes that it is dangerous for Val to stay, but the news of a child causes him to turn back to her.

Jabe appears on the stairs, firing a revolver into the store. Lady throws herself in front of Val and is hit twice. Jabe goes outside, shouting that the clerk has shot his wife and robbed the store. Val runs out through the confectionery. Men swarm into the store. Offstage, they catch Val. They take a blowtorch from the hardware section and direct its flames at Val. As the screams die out, the Conjure Man enters with the snakeskin jacket. Carol trades him a gold ring for it. She says: "Wild things leave skins behind them, they leave clean skins and teeth and white bones behind them, and these are tokens passed from one to another, so that the fugitive kind can always follow their kind. . . ."

In the earlier play, *Battle of Angels,* Jabe Torrance's wife is named Myra. There is no Italian father or wine garden in the past. More vulnerable than Lady, she allows herself to be cheated on goods by the towns-women. Cassandra Whiteside is the earlier incarnation of Carol Cutrere. In this play, much emphasis is placed upon her family's wealth, the revolver she carries, and the fact that her Greek namesake was a prophetess.

Val Xavier is younger in *Battle of Angels,* and he is a fugitive from the law in Texas. His attractiveness to women has caused all the difficulties in his life; this quality is dramatized when various townswomen come to buy shoes from him. A writer rather than a musician, he composes poems on shoe boxes and claims to be writing a book about life. He acquires a guitar only incidentally, late in the play, when he intercedes for a vagrant black, thus incurring the dislike of Sheriff Talbott and the other rednecks. The direct cause of Val's demise is the arrival in town of a revenge-bent woman from Waco whom Val had spurned. She enters just when the electricity goes out in the flood-threatend town. Led by her, the men carry pine torches into the confectionary and set it afire.

The published version of *Battle of Angels* has a Prologue and an Epilogue framing the main action with the perspective of one year's time since the oc-currence of the tragedy. The store has been converted into a museum, with the snakeskin jacket as a prize exhibit. The Temple sisters' explanation to a group of tourists reveal that in addition to Myra's having been shot and Val's death by fire, Cassandra drove her car into the rain-swollen river, and Vee Talbott went insane.

The biblical references in both versions of the play

are similar. The names Myra (an anagram of Mary) and Lady both suggest Our Lady, Mary the mother of God. In Act 1 of *Battle of Angels*, Myra calls Val "child" ("Lawd, child, come back in the mawning and I'll give you a job"), and he replies, "God, I—! Lady, you—!" Jabe is a surrogate husband, like Joseph. He and Myra/Lady are childless after at least ten years of marriage. The women, snooping upstairs while the Torrances are gone, learn that they have separate bedrooms at opposite ends of the hall.

That Val Xavier is a Christ figure is suggested by more than his name. Vee, with her mystical "visions," recognizes him as such. Val's stay in the corrupt Southern town may be likened to Christ's years on earth. Temptations are offered Val in Glorious Hill, and he resists, just as Christ spurned Satan on the mountaintop. Val's words and actions reveal compassion for humanity, including blacks and unknown convicts fleeing the chain-gang dogs. Of the book he is writing in *Battle of Angels*, he says: "It's got life in it, Myra. When people read it, they're going to be frightened. They'll say it's crazy because it tells the truth." Val suffers a passion and death at the hands of the townspeople. The snakeskin jacket he leaves behind, like Christ's shroud, suggests an Easter Sunday resurrection.

The change of title from *Battle of Angeles* to *Orpheus Descending* underscores the later play's more conscious application of Greek mythological materials. Carol Cutrere remains, despite her change of name, a doom-prophesying incarnation of the Greek Cassandra, who was able to foretell disaster but whose words were never taken seriously. In Act 2 of *Orpheus Descending*, she tells Val: "I drove all night to bring you this warning of danger." In Act 3, when she tells Lady that Val is leaving town, Lady replies: "You got some mighty wrong information." This subtle treatment more effectively evokes the Greek prototype than does the blatancy of Cassandra Whiteside in *Battle of Angels* with lines, accompanied by a flash of lightning, such as: "Behold, Cassandra, shouting doom at the gates!" In both plays, Vee Talbott may be likened to Tiresias, the holy blind seer of ancient Thebes who understood better than anyone else the will of the gods.

Orpheus of Greek mythology was a mortal who could charm the gods with his singing and playing of the lute. In *Orpheus Descending*, Williams makes Val a musician whose guitar is covered with autographs of the "immortals"— Leadbelly, Bessie Smith, Fats Waller, and others. Orpheus married Eurydice, but soon after the wedding she was bitten by a snake and died. The inconsolable Orpheus descended to the underworld and charmed its rulers into allowing Eurydice to return to earth on condition that he not turn to look back at her until they were outside the cavernous passage to Hades. In *Orpheus Descending,* Jabe is seen as Death, especially by Lady. When Jabe knocks for her with his cane on the floor above, Lady says to Val:

> Death's knocking for me! Don't you think I hear him, knock, knock, knock? It sounds like what it is! Bones knocking bones. . . . Ask me how it felt to be coupled with death up there, and I can tell you. My skin crawled when he touched me. But I endured it. I guess my heart knew that somebody must be coming to take me out of this hell! You did. You came. Now look at me! I'm alive once more!

There is also a clear parallel between Cerberus, the three-headed guard dog of the realm of death, and the three men who are so solicitous of Jabe: Sheriff Talbott, Dog, and PeeWee.

Just as Orpheus turned around too soon, before Eurydice had emerged from the cavern, Val pauses in his flight from Two River County when he learns that Lady is pregnant, and Death claims her again. The Greek Orpheus was torn to pieces by women, the handmaidens of Dionysus, in an orgiastic trance. Similarly, Val falls victim to an angry mob of towns-people. In the London production of *Orpheus Descending*, the ending was changed to establish that he was torn to pieces by an offstage pack of dogs.

The Theater Guild production of *Battle of Angels*, directed by Margaret Webster, opened its Boston try-out run on December 30, 1940. Many playgoers were offended by the frank language of the play; others laughed in the wrong places. Some were shocked, to the point of stalking out, at the scene in which Vee Talbott displays one of her paintings, a portrait of Christ resembling Val Xavier. At the opening night performance, the confectionery fire effects sent billows of smoke out into the auditorium, driving away still more of the audience before curtain call.

Boston city officials demanded cuts in the play, and Williams began working on revisions. Miriam Hopkins, who played Myra, defended the play ("I wouldn't be in it if it were a dirty play"), as did Lawrence Langner and Teresa Helburn in a letter to the Guild's Boston subscribers:

> In view of the unfortunate publicity caused by the Boston censor's protest about *Battle of Angels*, we feel it is only fair to give you the Guild's reasons for producing the play. We chose it because we felt the young author had genuine poetic gifts and an interesting insight into a particular

American scene. The treatment of the religious obsession of one of the characters, which sprang from frustration, did not justify in our opinion, the censor's action. It was, we felt, a sincere and honest attempt to present a true psychological picture.

Nevertheless, *Battle of Angels* closed in Boston on January 11, 1941, and the Theater Guild did not take up its option on the revised version submitted by Williams in 1942.

*Orpheus Descending* opened in New York on March 21, 1957, directed by Harold Clurman, with Maureen Stapleton as Lady and Cliff Robertson as Val. Williams felt that the critics had "put it down with a vengeance," but admitted in his *Memoirs* that the play was "overwritten." Most reviewers balanced their criticism of the loosely constructed story with appreciation for the beauty of Williams's language and for the "disturbing fascination" the play held for its "spellbound" audience (Richard Watts, *New York Post*). Tom Donnelly (*New York World-Telegram*) called it "the least characteristic of the author's plays," while John Chapman (*New York Daily News*) found it to be "like random samples of all Williams dramas and all of his characters."

A Paris production in March 1959 starred Arletty as Lady; critics were enthusiastic in welcoming her back to the stage after a long absence, but were less receptive to the play. Nor did it fare very well with critics of the May 1959 London production at the Royal Court Theater, directed by Tony Richardson. The play's greatest success was achieved by the production that opened in Moscow in August 1961. *Orpheus Descending* was the first of Williams's plays to be produced in the USSR, and it remained in the Mos-soviet Theater's repertory for seven years.

The film version, entitled *The Fugitive Kind*, directed by Sidney Lumet, was a disappointment in its first release, but has since acquired a cult following. The performances by Marlon Brando as Val and Anna Magnani as Lady are individually stunning, although not totally compatible. Brando's delivery of the lines about the transparent bird is a highlight of the film. This version culminates in Val's execution by both fire and water; he is pushed into the conflagration in the confectionery by the force of the water from the firehoses which the townspeople direct at him.

## 18. The Glass Menagerie

*The Glass Menagerie* was Williams's first play to reach Broadway, and it was a triumph. Referring to the very different fortunes of this play and of *Battle of Angels* four years earlier, Williams reportedly said, "You can't mix sex and religion . . . but you can always write safely about mothers."

Although the characterization of the mother is generally perceived as unsympathetic, *The Glass Menagerie* is Williams's gentlest play. This is because the mother, Amanda Wingfield, and her daughter Laura are so isolated in their personal illusions of life. Amanda's son Tom, the narrator-protagonist, attempts to convey a sense of the harsh realistic background against which their story is set: "the slow and implacable fires of human desperation," hot swing music and liquor, labor disputes and economic depression in America, and Berchtesgaden and Guernica in Europe. But Tom is the only one of the three to make contact with that outer reality, and even he prefers the escapism of the movies.

The play is composed of scenes from Tom's memory, filtered through his remembered desire to escape from his mother's apartment and from his shoe-factory warehouse job, and through his implicit feelings of guilt for actually having abandoned his sister. "In the episodic play such as this," Williams wrote in his production notes, "the basic structure or narrative line may be obscured from the audience; the effect may seem fragmentary rather than architectural." This fragmentary quality is justified by the selectivity of memory and by the fact that each fragment is so finely chiselled. It is easy to see why Williams has been called a good "scenewright." So tightly written are the scenes in *The Glass Menagerie*, so full of musicality and suggestive power are the lines of dialogue, so integral are the effects of sound and lighting—that a summation of what is said and done on stage cannot nearly convey a sense of the play.

The formal division of the play consists of seven scenes. Scenes 1–5 are entitled "Preparation for a Gentleman Caller," and Scenes 6 and 7, "The Gentleman Calls." The scene divisions are not apparent to the audience, since most scenes are in turn composed of shorter episodes, and all segments are linked by changes in the lighting and by a "recurring tune, which dips in and out of the play as if it were carried on a wind that changes."

In Williams's original conception of the play, the setting was to incorporate a screen on which images and titles would be projected, to give emphasis to certain values in each episode. These images and titles are specified in library editions of the play (New Directions and most anthologies), but not in the acting edition (Dramatists Play Service). The screen device was not included in the original production, nor is it generally used, although it might be useful to enhance the conceptual unity of other nonrealistic elements of the play. For example, as if in answer to Tom's questioning the possibility of escape, the grinning wall photograph of his long-absent father lights up.

Tom begins the play by strolling onto the fire escape outside the Wingfields' St. Louis tenement apartment. He addresses the audience:

> Yes, I have tricks in my pocket, I have things up my sleeve. But I am the opposite of a stage magician. He gives you illusion that has the appearance of truth. I give you truth in the pleasant disguise of illusion.

He explains that the play is memory. Then he enters the apartment as the lights come up on the interior. His first memory is of his mother Amanda thrusting upon her children the recollections and values of her long-lost way of life among the planters of the Mississippi Delta. She tells about the Sunday afternoon when she received seventeen gentlemen callers, and she tactlessly reproaches her daughter Laura for not having any.

Amanda learns that Laura has stopped going to classes at Rubicam's Business College because Laura is so shy about the brace she wears on one leg. Now that it is apparent that Laura will never be in a position to support herself, Amanda becomes obsessed with the idea of finding "some nice young man" to marry Laura. "Realizing that extra money would be needed to properly feather the nest and plume the bird," Amanda begins selling magazine subscriptions by telephone. Two of her hysterically eloquent sales pitches intersperse the action.

An argument with Tom brings forth more eloquence. One example is the speech in which she repeats the word "movies" and in which the "m" and "n" sounds take on the incantatory effect of poetry:

> I don't believe that you go every night to the movies. Nobody goes to the movies night after night. Nobody in their right mind goes to the movies as often as you pretend to. People don't go to the movies at midnight, and movies don't let out at two A.M. Come in stumbling. Muttering to yourself like a maniac! You get three hours sleep and then go to work. Oh, I can picture the way you're doing down there. Moping, doping because you're in no condition.

Tom's anger builds to the point at which he calls his mother an "ugly—babbling old—*witch*" and hurls his coat across the room. His coat strikes the shelf that holds Laura's glass collection. Amanda exits, declaring that she will not speak to Tom again until he apologizes. Tom crosses the room and kneels to pick up the pieces of glass.

The next morning, in response to Laura's plea, Tom apologizes to Amanda. On speaking terms again, they nearly resume the same quarrel, but, with Laura sent out on an errand, Amanda succeeds in having Tom agree to bring home some nice young man from the warehouse to meet Laura.

After supper one evening, Tom casually tells Amanda that he is bringing someone home to dinner the following day. Amanda begins a flurry of questions about the young man's character, background, and prospects for the future. Tom cautions her that the gentleman caller doesn't know about Laura, nor should Amanda expect too much of Laura: "She lives in a world of little glass ornaments, Mother. . . . She plays old phonograph records and—that's about all—." He leaves for the movies. Amanda calls Laura from the kitchen to wish on the moon.

The dinner guest, Jim O'Connor, had been a high-school hero six years before. He was the boy whom Laura secretly liked in high school. At the warehouse, he is Tom's only friend. He knows of Tom's habit of retiring to the washroom to write poems on the lids of shoe boxes. When Laura learns that Jim is to be the guest, she becomes nervous and ill. She panics and bolts from the room after answering the door. Amanda appears, wearing a girlish frock resurrected from a trunk—the dress she was wearing when she met her husband. She lavishes her Southern charm on Jim and credits Laura with having cooked the dinner. Too ill to come to the table with the others, Laura is left lying on the living room sofa.

Just as dinner is ending, all the lights in the apartment go out; Tom had neglected to pay the electric bill. He and Amanda go to the kitchen, while Jim is sent into the parlor, carrying a candelabrum with lighted candles, to entertain Laura. Jim tells Laura about the courses he is taking for self-improvement and about his plans to get in on the ground floor of television and go right to the top with it. He judges her to be an "old-fashioned type of girl" which he thinks is "a pretty good type to be." Gradually, Jim draws her out, and, finally she shows him her collection of little glass animals.

Jim asks Laura to dance with him to the music coming from the Paradise Dance Hall across the alley. While dancing, they knock to the floor Laura's favorite glass animal—the unicorn. With its horn broken off, Laura assures Jim that it will feel less "freakish." Clearly, Jim has had this effect on Laura too. After he kisses her and then awkwardly apologizes, explaining that he cannot "do the right thing," cannot take down her phone number and "call up next week" because he is already engaged to be married, she gives him the hornless unicorn as a "souvenir."

Amanda enters with a pitcher of lemonade and learns of Jim's engagement. As soon as Jim has left, Amanda turns against Tom to reproach him for the fact that they had entertained "some other girl's fiancé." Tom starts to make his habitual escape to the movies, and Amanda says, "Go then! Go to the moon—you selfish dreamer!" And Tom tells the audience:

> I didn't go to the moon, I went much further—for time is the longest distance between two places. . . . I would have stopped, but I was pursued by something. It always came upon me unawares, taking me altogether by surprise. Perhaps it was a familiar bit of music. Perhaps it was only a piece of transparent glass. Perhaps I am walking along a street at night, in some strange city, before I have found companions. I pass the lighted window of a shop where perfume is sold. The window is filled with pieces of colored glass, tiny transparent bottles in delicate colors, like bits of shattered rainbow. Then all at once my sister touches my shoulder. I turn around and look into her eyes. Oh, Laura, Laura, I tried to leave you behind me, but I am more faithful than I intended to be! I reach for a cigarette, I cross the street, I run into the movies or a bar, I buy a drink, I speak to the nearest stranger—anything that can blow your candles out! . . . For nowadays the world is lit by lightning! Blow out your candles, Laura—and so goodbye. . . .

*The Glass Menagerie* is sometimes called an expressionist play, but it is probably closer to symbolist drama, with its poetic language, suggestive interplay of *états d'âme*, and use of light and music to play upon the sensibilities. It has been called naturalistic, as well as Chekhovian. Like Chekhov's plays, it has been staged both as comedy and as tragedy. It sets up contrasts between the dreamer (Tom) and the doer (Jim), past and present, fantasy and actuality, desire for escape and awareness of responsibility, psychological and physical handicaps, a civilization "gone with the wind" and a world obsessed with technological progress. It can be seen as a play about conflict between generations, posing the question that Williams later articulated in his *Memoirs* and hinted at in several other plays: "Why do women bring children into the world and then destroy them?" Clive Barnes (*New York Times*, December 19, 1975) has called *The Glass Menagerie* a play about loss and survival. Roger B. Stein, in his essay "*The Glass Menagerie* Revisited: Catastrophe without Violence" (in *Tennessee Williams: A Collection of Critical Essays*), discusses its extensive religious imagery and symbolism. In broadest terms, *The Glass Menagerie* is a dramatic poem about human nature.

*The Glass Menagerie* was first produced at the Civic Theater in Chicago on December 26, 1944, with set design and lighting by Jo Mielziner and original music composed by Paul Bowles. Eddie Dowling was producer and director, and he played the role of Tom. The role of Amanda was taken by Laurette Taylor, in a comeback after a long absence from the stage. She had virtually dropped out of sight after the death of her husband J. Hartley Manners in 1928, and was remembered most fondly for her creation of the title role in his play *Peg o' My Heart* in 1912. Her name was soon to become as closely associated with Amanda Wingfield as it had been, for an earlier generation of theatergoers, with Peg. In 1944, it was considered somewhat of a risk to cast her at all, but her rightness in the part became legendary.

Chicago critics wrote glowing reviews of the play and of its performers, but, perhaps because of the icy weather, the public ignored the production. After the first week's disappointing box office, Dowling and coproducer Louis J. Singer decided to close the play, but Chicago newspaper critics launched a crusade to save it. Claudia Cassidy, Ashton Stevens, Henry T. Murdock, and others used their daily columns to urge theatergoers not to let a work of art of such rare quality die in Chicago. The press used its power to good effect, for in the third week of its Chicago run, *The Glass Menagerie* began playing to full houses.

That same production opened at the Playhouse Theater in New York on March 31, 1945, and New York critics echoed the rave reviews of Chicago. Julie Hayden as Laura, Anthony Ross as the Gentleman Caller, and Eddie Dowling all received a share of the praise. There was special appreciation for "one of the most amazing love scenes ever written," a scene ending with the gentleman going happily away forever.

Many critics were at a loss for words to evoke Laurette Taylor's "truly great performance." Their attempts to recapture it suggest a complexity of subtle shadings in which humor and pathos were "beautifully mated." Louis Kronenberger (*New York Newspaper PM*) wrote: "She nags, she flutters, she flatters, she coaxes, she pouts, she fails to understand, she understands all too well—all this revealed, most of the time, in vague little movements and half-mumbled words, small changes of pace, faint shifts of emphasis, little rushes of energy and masterfulness, quiet droopings of spirit." According to Lewis Nichols (*New York Times*):

> Miss Taylor takes these good passages and makes them sing. She plays softly and part of the time seems to be mumbling—a mumble that can be heard at the top of the gallery. Her accents, like the author's phrases, are unexpected; her gestures are vague and fluttery. There is no doubt she was a Southern belle; there is no doubt she is a great actress.

Helen Hayes, by contrast, in the November 1956 revival, "doesn't quite make you believe in the mother's lost days as a Dixie belle as vividly as Miss Taylor did, but she is wonderfully moving, nevertheless" (Richard Watts, Jr., *New York Post*). According to Walter Kerr (*New York Herald Tribune*), "Miss Hayes plays it like a belligerant sparrow bent on marching her brood right into kingdom-come. She is a battling bantam cock bashing at the world in an untidy bathrobe . . . not so much a grinding echo of glories long lost as a foolish shining faith in glories yet to come."

In the spring of 1961, Miss Hayes led a specially assembled troupe under State Department auspices on a fifteen-week tour of Europe and the Middle East. The three plays toured by this American Repertory Company were *The Glass Menagerie*, Thornton Wilder's *The Skin of Our Teeth,* and William Gibson's *The Miracle Worker*. They were generally received with standing ovations from capacity audiences and with overwhelmingly enthusiastic critical acclaim. Among the cities visited were Madrid, Rome, Vienna, Ankara, Tel-Aviv, Athens, Beirut, Berlin, Stockholm, Helsinki, Copenhagen, and Paris. The

success of that tour led to a thirteen-week tour of the
three plays to fifteen Latin American cities in the fall
of 1961.

In May 1965, Maureen Stapleton portrayed Amanda
on Broadway. Like Helen Hayes nine years earlier,
she was subjected to comparisons with the memory
of Laurette Taylor and was found wanting in ability
to suggest "the sense of a charmed past—whether
imaginary or real. . . . Miss Stapleton seems to live
fully in St. Louis, not half in a dream" (Walter Kerr,
*New York Times*). Her performance was considered
honest, appealing, and nuanced.

Maureen Stapleton recreated the role of Amanda
ten years later at the Circle in the Square Theater, in
a production that several reviewers felt did not do
justice to the play. Martin Gottfried (*New York Post*)
reported that the director had "reduced it to second-
rate naturalism." Edwin Wilson (*Wall Street Journal*)
said that the production provided the "broad outlines
and the inevitable high points, "but neglected the
"underground rhythm of the scenes," "these modula-
tions, these nuances—the music, if you will."

A highly acclaimed American Broadcasting Company television production of *The Glass Menagerie*
was presented on December 16, 1973. Williams was
pleased to see Tom's narrative speeches cut down in
length. Katharine Hepburn's portrayal of Amanda,
said Harry F. Waters (*Newsweek*, December 17, 1973),
"almost makes you forget that anyone else ever tried.
. . . She not only vocally captures the mother's humor,
fragility, and steel, but she  fleshes out the impact
with that special Hepburn body language." Completing the cast were Sam Waterston as Tom, Joanna
Miles as Laura, and Michael Moriarty as the Gentleman Caller. The latter choice was termed an "inspira-
tion. . . . He peels away the caller's cocky patina; and

we see a vulnerable extrovert, the high-school athlete who has learned the unreliability of year-book prophecies."

Gertrude Lawrence played Amanda for high comedy in the 1950 film version of *The Glass Menagerie*. A number of specific distortions in the screenplay of the subtle values of the play are discussed in Maurice Yacowar's *Tennessee Williams and Film*. Williams reiterated earlier critical opinion when, in 1973, he called the film "the most awful travesty of the play I've ever seen."

## 19. You Touched Me!

In New York from March through May 1942, Williams collaborated with Donald Windham on drafting a dramatization of D.H. Lawrence's short story "You Touched Me." The play is set in an English country house, part of which is fitted out like the interior of a ship—the last command of Captain Rockley. Fortified by drink, he holds out against the encroaching feminine gentility of the rest of the house. His sister Emmie is a prudish spinster who has so dominated the Captain's daughter Matilda that this delicate young girl of twenty seems colorless and dispirited. Young Hadrian, however, is attracted to Matilda and tries to find a way of freeing her repressed sensibilities. A breakthrough occurs when Matilda enters her father's room in the dark to say goodnight, not knowing that Hadrian is using her father's bed, and she touches Hadrian's forehead. For another act and a half, Emmie's machinations to keep both Matilda and the Captain under her self-righteous domination thwart the young people's attraction to each other, but a Lawrencian instinct for life finally triumphs.

After the first draft was written, Williams left New York. Work on revisions continued for the rest of the year by correspondence with Windham. In June Williams injected into the action a symbolic fox-raid on the hen coop. In October, following Audrey Wood's advice, he gave the play a "contemporary significance" by setting it during the war and by giving Hadrian, now a Royal Air Force lieutenant on leave, some idealistic speeches about the postwar world.

Margo Jones directed a production of the play in Cleveland during October 1943 and took it to Pasadena in November. Not until after the Broadway success of *The Glass Menagerie* was there any interest in bringing *You Touched Me!* to New York. Then, directed by Guthrie McClintic and featuring Montgomery Clift as Hadrian (now a Royal Canadian Air Force flyer, to explain his accent), it opened at the Booth Theater on September 25, 1945. It ran for 109 performances, closing January 5, 1946.

Reviewers tended to see the play as "a hopelessly confused patchwork," which included "everything from poetry to farce, from lecture platform harangues to several one-man comedy turns for Edmund Gwenn, cast as an old sea captain" (Wilella Waldorf, *New York Post*). Gwenn's performance, enlivened by his imitations of the fox and chicken and by his tale of a female porpoise who once made amorous advances to him, was the most appreciated aspect of the production.

## 20. A Streetcar Named Desire

*A Streetcar Named Desire* is a lyrical drama about the decline and fall of Blanche DuBois. It was in terms of Blanche that director Elia Kazan analyzed the dramatic action in each of the play's eleven scenes in his private rehearsal notebook (published in *Directors on Directing*, Toby Cole and Helen Crich Chinoy, editors) for the original 1947 production. Blanche is often regarded as a symbol of decaying tradition, beauty, and refinement pitted in a losing battle against the crude vitality of the progressive mainstream. Yet, the audience sees her operate as a liar, a pretentious hypocrite, a near-alcoholic, a seductress of young boys, a disrupter of a stable, "normal" household. Although Blanche has impressed critics as anything from a figure of tragic stature to an object of ridicule, she has clearly established herself as the "first lady" of American dramatic literature.

The setting, showing both the exterior and interior of a two-story house in New Orleans, establishes an atmosphere of decadent charm with its "tender blue" sky, "warm breath of the brown river" nearby, "easy intermingling of races," and "Blue Piano" music from a bar around the corner. The women seated on the outside stairs that connect the upstairs and downstairs apartments are exchanging vulgarities when Blanche enters. She is a dainty woman in her thirties, dressed all in white and fluttering with uncertainty like a moth. She says she had taken a streetcar named Desire and then transferred to one called Cemeteries, a subtle adumbration of her movement in the play from longing to annihilation. Now she is looking for her sister Stella—Mrs. Stanley Kowalski. Eunice, who lives upstairs, shows Blanche into the downstairs flat, then goes to fetch Stella from the bowling alley. Left alone, Blanche finds a whiskey bottle and quickly takes a drink.

The reunion of the two sisters allows a skillful integration of background information and character revelation in the dialogue. It is readily apparent that

Blanche's domination of Stella and her cadging for compliments are integral to their relationship. Blanche reveals her hypocrisy when she pretends to search for something to drink. She expresses her disappointment with Stella's untidy two-room apartment, but hints at how badly she needs it as a place of refuge.

Blanche is evasive in explaining why she has arrived before the end of the spring term at the school in Laurel where she has been teaching English, and she is defensive while breaking the news to Stella that they have lost Belle Reve, the plantation where both girls grew up. Becoming hysterical, she recalls the horror of living with the sickness and death of each member of the family, "the long parade to the graveyard," and the cost of the funerals. The gathering force of her monologue drives Stella into the bathroom to wash her face, and Blanche is left to meet Stanley alone.

Stanley sizes Blanche up quickly. He uses his vulgarity to test and manipulate her. For the second time in Scene 1, a cat screeches near the window, startling Blanche and now summoning up a cat-and-mouse image for the relationship of Stanley and Blanche. The scene ends with Stanley asking Blanche about her youthful marriage. Over a faint strain of polka music, she replies: "The boy—the boy died. I'm afraid I'm—going to be sick!"

In Scene 2, the following evening, Stanley learns of the loss of Belle Reve. While Blanche soaks in a hot tub to quiet her nerves, Stanley pulls dresses and jewelry out of Blanche's trunk to convince Stella that she has been swindled out of her share of the estate. Under Louisiana's Napoleonic code, he tells her, if she has been swindled, so has he. Blanche emerges from her bath and sends Stella to the drugstore to get a lemon coke. She finds that Stanley is immune to her

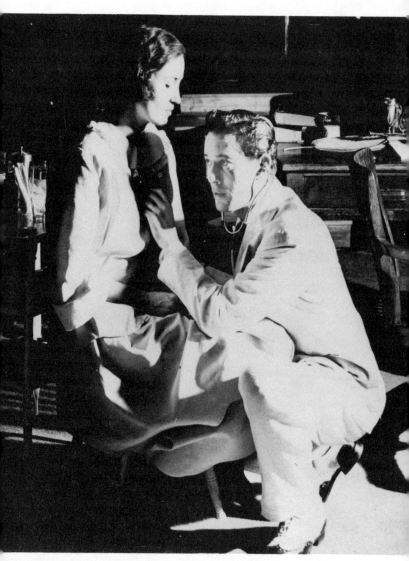

In July 1947 Margo Jones, the "Texas tornado," directed the original production of *Summer and Smoke* in her arena-stage Theater '47 in Dallas. Katharine Balfour and Tod Andrews created the roles of Alma Winemiller and John Buchanan.

A German interpretation of Blanche DuBois and Stanley Kowalski is shown in this photograph from a production of *A Streetcar Named Desire* at the State Theater in Regensburg, Germany.

GERMAN INFORMATION CENTER

Soviet actor A. Dzhigarkhanyan and actress S.V. Nemoyaeva
played Stanley and Blanche at the Mayakovsky Theater in
Moscow in 1971. There have been a number of productions
of *A Streetcar Named Desire* in the USSR; this one was
directed by A. Goncharov.

TASS FROM SOVFOTO

*Opposite*, The Moscow Art Theater produced *Sweet Bird of Youth* in 1975, claiming that "the play shows the life of simple, contemporary American people." It was directed by People's Actor O. Efremov. Pictured are USSR People's Actress A. Stepanova as Alexandra Del Lago and I. Vasilyev as Chance Wayne.

*Kingdom of Earth* was retitled *The Knightly Quest* for the 1978 production at the Mossoviet Theater in Moscow. Valentina Talyzina and Georgy Zhzhenov played Myrtle and Chicken.

Al Pacino played Kilroy in the 1970 revival of *Camino Real* at the Vivian Beaumont Theater of Lincoln Center, New York. Gutman is visible in the background, fanning himself on the terrace of the Siete Mares Hotel.

MARTHA SWOPE

In his *New York Times* review of the 1974 American Shakespeare Theater revival of *Cat on a Hot Tin Roof*, Clive Barnes praised Elizabeth Ashley's "sensuous, withdrawn, composed, and determined" Maggie. He wrote that she "vibrantly combines charm with grit" and that "Keir Dullea's ironic, embittered Brick makes her the perfect partner."

MARTHA SWOPE

Tennessee Williams poses in the foreground with the cast of *Small Craft Warnings* at the Truck and Warehouse Theater in 1972. Cherry Davis was a red-headed Violet, and Helena Carroll played Leona Dawson.

MARTHA SWOPE

coquettish airs, but she blithely presents him with all of the papers relating to the estate. In a single momentary deviation from her mood of gaiety in this scene, Blanche withholds a faded, ribbon-tied sheaf of love-letters: "Poems a dead boy wrote. I hurt him the way that you would like to hurt me, but you can't! I'm not young and vulnerable any more. But my young husband was. . . ." Stanley says he has a "lawyer acquaintance" who will study the papers, since it is especially important now that Stella is going to have a baby.

At that news, Blanche goes to meet Stella on the sidewalk and tells her that maybe Stanley is "what we need to mix with our blood now that we've lost Belle Reve." (Since "belle" is the feminine form of the adjective "beautiful" in French, whereas "rêve"— "dream"—is a masculine noun, it seems probable that the estate was originally called Belle Rive—"beautiful shore"—and that the corruption of the name is symbolic of the tenuousness of its reality by the time it has come down to Blanche's generation.) The sisters go off to dinner and a show, as Stanley's friends arrive for an evening of poker.

Scene 3 is the only one given a title: The Poker Night. The game is still going on when Blanche and Stella return after two in the morning. Beer bottles and watermelon rinds litter the kitchen floor. Blanche notices that Mitch, a bachelor, seems somewhat "superior to the others." She asks him to put a colored paper lantern over the bedroom light bulb: "I can't stand a naked light bulb, any more than I can a rough word or a vulgar action." She turns on the radio and they begin to dance, but Stanley, enraged, storms into the bedroom and pitches the radio out the window. Stella cries, "Drunk—drunk—animal thing, you," and

Stanley charges to attack her. The men drag Stanley into the shower, while Blanche leads Stella to Eunice's apartment upstairs.

When Stanley comes out of the shower, his apartment is deserted. He telephones Eunice upstairs, then stumbles out to the foot of the stairs and bawls: "Stell–lahhhhh!" Eunice yells insults down at him and slams her door. Stanley howls again. This time, Stella softly descends to embrace him. He carries her into their darkened apartment.

Blanche descends hesitantly. She recoils, as if struck, when she senses the extent to which she has been excluded from the haven of Stella's apartment. To Mitch, who fortuitously reappears and invites her to sit on the steps for a cigarette with him, Blanche hints at her desperation: "Thank you for being so kind! I need kindness now."

The next morning a distraught Blanche confronts her sister, who is contentedly lolling in bed. Blanche cannot comprehend Stella's tolerance for this kind of life or her love for a man who has only "animal force" to offer. The scene builds to Blanche's long speech, a hysterically eloquent direct attack on Stanley. Unseen by both women, Stanley has entered the kitchen and overhears Blanche describing him as an apelike "survivor of the stone age." Invoking the world's progress by means of art, poetry, music, and "tenderer feelings," Blanche begs Stella: "Don't—don't hang back with the brutes." Stanley goes out stealthily, then calls Stella from outside, and reenters. Grease-stained though Stanley is, Stella rushes to embrace him. Over Stella's shoulder, Stanley grins triumphantly at Blanche.

Scene 5 occurs late on a hot August afternoon, punctuated with thunder and lightning. Stanley hints that he has learned something unsavory about Blanche's reputation in Laurel, the town she has come from. Blanche realizes that she will not long continue to find sanctuary in Stella's home; she confides to Stella her hope that she can get Mitch to marry her. Blanche is waiting alone in the apartment for Mitch when a Young Man comes to collect for the newspaper. Blanche has no money, but she flirts with the boy and longingly kisses him on the mouth. Then she sends him away, saying, "I've got to be good—and keep my hands off children."

Home from their late evening date, Blanche has a long scene with Mitch. Her role-playing, evasiveness, and pretensions are etched against his good-hearted simplicity. Blanche tells Mitch about the boy she married when she was sixteen. Distant polka music is heard as she recalls how, on the dance floor, she confronted her young husband with her discovery of his homosexuality: "I saw! I know! You disgust me." The boy then ran outside and shot himself. Moved by her story, Mitch proposes to Blanche.

It is on Blanche's birthday in mid-September that Stanley tells Stella that he has obtained proof of Blanche's shady past. He has learned that she was fired from her high-school teaching job for getting involved with a seventeen-year-old boy, and she was even asked to move out of Laurel's infamous Hotel Flamingo. Stella refuses to believe these stories. She continues preparations for the birthday party, while Blanche warbles "a saccharine popular ballad" in the bathroom.

In Scene 8, about an hour later, the birthday supper is almost over. Blanche, with forced gaiety, tells a joke to cover her anxiety over Mitch's not having shown up. Stella comments on Stanley's vulgar table manners. He reacts by throwing dishes on the floor and stalking out. While Blanche tries unsuccessfully to telephone Mitch, Stella joins Stanley on the porch. He talks of how everything will be all right again once Blanche has left and they can "get the colored lights going" again. When they are all reassembled in the kitchen for the birthday cake, Stanley gives Blanche a "little birthday remembrance"—a bus ticket back to Laurel for the following Tuesday. Blanche tries to laugh, but precipitously bolts for the bathroom. Protesting Stanley's cruelty, Stella suddenly realizes that she needs to be taken to the hospital.

Later that evening, Blanche is alone, drinking to escape the polka music in her mind. Mitch arrives and tears the paper lantern off the light bulb to get a good look at Blanche, since she has never let him see her in daylight. "I don't want realism. I want magic! . . . I don't tell truth, I tell what *ought* to be truth," she says. Seeing that Mitch has found out about her past, she gives him the most truthful explanation she can of her intimacies with strangers: she sought protection and to fill her empty heart after the death of her boy husband.

A Mexican street vendor comes to the door offering "flores para los muertos"—flowers for the dead. Blanche recoils and loses herself in recollections of the deaths with which she has had to cope. She dealt with death by seeking its opposite: desire. Mitch grapples with her, saying he will no longer marry her, but he wants "what I been missing all summer." Blanche rushes to the window and calls, "Fire!" until Mitch leaves. She falls to her knees.

When Scene 10 opens, it is several hours later. Blanche is dressed in a white satin evening gown, silver slippers, and a rhinestone tiara. Stanley enters. He came home because the baby is not due before morning. As Blanche prattles to him about a telegram from her old boyfriend Shep Huntleigh, inviting her for a cruise on his yacht, it becomes apparent that

Blanche has retreated into her last possible refuge, the fantasy-world of her own mind. But Stanley denies her even that solace; he exposes her face-saving "lies and deceit and tricks." Her mounting panic is given a scenic metaphor: "Lurid reflections appear on the wall around Blanche. The shadows are of grotesque and menacing form. . . . The night is filled with inhuman voices like cries in a jungle." Her terror seems to challenge Stanley. He moves toward her. She smashes a bottle in order to ward him off with the broken end, but he overpowers her and carries her to the bed, saying: "We've had this date with each other from the beginning!"

Some weeks later, Stella is packing Blanche's things in the bedroom while Stanley and friends play poker in the kitchen. While Blanche calls instructions from the bedroom, Stella tells Eunice she's not sure they're doing the right thing, but she couldn't believe Blanche's story and go on living with Stanley. However, Blanche has affected their lives more profoundly than they realize. Mitch has lost all tolerance for Stanley's braggart machismo. Eunice regards the poker players as insensitive "pigs." Stella, now a mother, has become fully conscious of her own plight.

Blanche dresses to meet Shep Huntleigh. A Doctor and a Matron come to the door. Stella accompanies Blanche through the kitchen. This time, in contrast to The Poker Night, the men stand. When Blanche sees that her caller is not Shep Huntleigh, she rushes back to the bedroom. Stanley follows, taunting her with having forgotten something: he tears the paper lantern off the light bulb to give to her. According to the stage directions, "she cries out as if the lantern was herself." Symbolically, it was herself—a flimsy bit of magic endeavoring to transform the hardness of reality. Blanche tries to run back out, but the Matron restrains her. The Doctor approaches Blanche in a more humane manner. He offers his arm. "Whoever you are—I have always depended on the kindness of strangers," Blanche says, as she allows him to lead her away.

At the poker table, Mitch has collapsed in sobs. On the porch, Stella cries out after her sister and weeps uncontrollably. The fact that Stella has not spoken a word to Stanley in the entire scene and has expressed concern only for her baby and Blanche seemingly belies the play's final image of the united family: Stanley, Stella, and, wrapped in a blue blanket, their baby.

A retelling of the dramatic action does not, of course, do justice to the nuance and variety in *A Streetcar Named Desire*. Each scene includes specific instructions for the blues piano, clarinet, brasses, train noises, and street vendors' cries that comment upon Blanche's drama. As in all of Williams's serious plays, there are comic moments, like Stella's line in the following interchange, which never fails to elicit laughter in performance:

> BLANCHE: Well, honey, a shot never does a coke any harm! Let me! You mustn't wait on me!
> STELLA: I like to wait on you, Blanche. It makes it seem more like home.

There is, in addition, an elaborate network of symbolism. Leonard Quirino has written at length (in *Tennessee Williams: A Tribute*) on the symbols connected with the card game and with the water imagery surrounding Blanche. A very early draft of the play was entitled *The Primary Colors*, the colors associated with Stanley and the poker game. Blanche, in contrast, is drawn to "soft colors, the colors of butterfly wings." For her final departure, Blanche wears, on her Della Robbia blue jacket, a bunch of artificial violets. Her hope that Mitch would be "a cleft in the rock of the world that I could hide in" had not come true. It remained for Williams to vindicate Blanche with his later play *Camino Real*, in which "the violets in the mountains break the rocks."

Reviewers for the original 1947 production wrote favorably of the play and of its direction by Elia Kazan. Several critics compared *A Streetcar Named Desire* with Williams's success of two years earlier and found the new work "an enormous advance" over *The Glass Menagerie*. The cast was well balanced with Jessica Tandy as Blanche, Marlon Brando as Stanley, Kim Hunter as Stella, and Karl Malden as Mitch.

Produced in London in October 1949, *A Streetcar Named Desire* aroused such controversy that the *London Evening Standard* announced that it would publish the entire text of the play in serial form. In Paris at the same time, the play, which was adapted by Jean Cocteau, pleased its audiences, but was severely denounced by the critics.

For the 1951 film version, Elia Kazan directed the New York cast in the same major roles, with the exception of Blanche—now played by Vivien Leigh, who had done the part in the London stage production. Despite a number of minor changes from the stage version, including an ending in which Stella seems to reject Stanley and retreats upstairs with her baby, the film is a sensitive rendering of the play. It is also an outstanding motion picture, recognized by the American Film Institute as one of the fifty all-time great American movies. Marlon Brando's projection of animal exuberance is exquisitely matched by Vivien

Leigh's evocation of decadent gentility. Vivien Leigh, Kim Hunter, and Karl Malden won Academy Awards for their performances.

The 1956 New York revival was hampered by the miscasting of Tallulah Bankhead as Blanche. Critics found her sincere in her approach to the role and utterly fascinating, but the play was diminished by the strength of her personality. Other notable interpretations of Blanche and Stanley were those of Uta Hagen and Anthony Quinn in 1949, of Rosemary Harris and James Farentino in the 1973 twenty-fifth anniversary production in New York, and of Faye Dunaway and Jon Voight, who (on the same occasion) played the roles in Los Angeles. Claire Bloom played Blanche in a 1974 London revival.

## 21. *Summer and Smoke* and *Eccentricities of a Nightingale*

Conflict between spiritual and corporeal needs in human existence might be perceived as the crux of a number of Williams's plays (*You Touched Me!, A Streetcar Named Desire, The Rose Tattoo, Camino Real*, and *The Night of the Iguana* are a few examples), but nowhere is this conflict treated with such heavy-handed symbolism as in *Summer and Smoke*. During the play, one is reminded four times that Alma's name is Spanish for soul; her father, Reverend Winemiller, ministers to men's spirits. The parlor of the rectory occupies one side of the stage, and the interior of Dr. Buchanan's office in his home occupies the other. The doctor's ministry to the body is symbolized by a large anatomy chart.

Between these two interior settings is the public drinking fountain in the town's main park. The fountain is in the form of a stone angel whose hands form a cup from which water flows; its wings are lifted toward the great expanse of sky, which is described in the stage directions as crucial to the play. In contrast to the angel's heavenward orientation, those who drink at the fountain in the course of the play are seen to be seeking sensual fulfillment. The town's name, Glorious Hill, suggests the aspirations of the spirit—up from the earth toward glory. But the town also has its Moon Lake Casino, a place associated in many of Williams's plays with the pitfalls of the flesh.

A Prologue, which is omitted from the acting edition of the play, shows Alma Winemiller and John Buchanan as children in the early 1900s. John attacks Alma with a peashooter, because she had embarrassed him in school with a gift box of handkerchiefs. The handkerchief—small, white, and fluttery like Alma herself—is used throughout the play as an image for her character, while the ring she nervously twists on her finger represents her never-to-be-fulfilled dream of marriage. The leitmotiv for John is an offstage voice calling "Johnny, Johnny!" The spirit/body dichotomy is suggested in the Prologue by Alma's emotional association with the stone angel, named "Eternity," to which John is indifferent. He teases Alma, seizes and kisses her, and runs away.

The remaining twelve scenes, evenly divided into two parts—"A Summer" and "A Winter"—take place when the two are in their twenties, shortly before the first World War. Alma teaches singing and helps her father to bear his "Cross," Mrs. Winemiller, who has regressed to behaving like a querulous and perverse child. John has completed his medical studies, but his constant drinking, gambling, and womanizing have earned the elder Dr. Buchanan's strong displeasure. (In the acting edition, this is revealed in a scene,

omitted from the library edition, between Alma and
Dr. Buchanan in his office.)

Home for the summer, John flirts with the nervous,
breathless Alma in a casual encounter by the fountain during the town's Fourth of July celebration.
Against a sky full of fireworks, she lectures him on the
responsibilities that go with his profession. John invites her to go riding in his automobile some afternoon.

> ALMA. Would you observe the speed limit?
> JOHN. Strictly with you, Miss Alma.
> ALMA. Why, then, I'd be glad to—John.
> JOHN. And wear a hat with a plume!
> ALMA. I don't have a hat with a plume!
> JOHN. Get one!

John drinks at the fountain and exits to follow Rose
Gonzales, a "fast" girl whose father owns Moon Lake
Casino.

The plume is symbolic of liberation from societal
constraints, for in the next scene, Mrs. Winemiller is
found to have shoplifted a white plumed hat. Alma
threatens to return it if her mother doesn't behave
herself during Alma's literary club meeting that
evening. Alma telephones John to cajole him, in her
light, affected manner, into attending the meeting.
Alma's singing pupil Nellie stops in and confides to
Alma that she has a crush on "Doctor Johnny." Mrs.
Winemiller babbles to Nellie that Alma is in love with
the young doctor and spies on him from the parlor
window. As soon as Nellie leaves, Alma, angered by
the embarrassment, fights with her mother. They tear
the plumed hat between them.

The club-meeting scene is high comedy. John
quickly flees the odd assortment of social eccentrics

gathered in the rectory parlor. Alma, scarcely hiding her feelings for John, scolds the group in a manner that subtly echoes her mother's. The meeting adjourns quickly. That same night, at 2:00 A.M., Alma knocks at the doctor's office. John is inside with Rosa Gonzales. He tells Rosa to wait outside. Alma insists that she must see John's father who often prescribes sleeping tablets to calm her. She nervously obeys John's instructions to unbutton her blouse, so that he can listen to her heart. All he hears is a little voice saying, "Miss Alma is lonesome!" He gives her some tablets and says he will call for her at eight o'clock on Saturday. Rosa reenters as Alma leaves. The light dims on all of the scene, except on the anatomy chart before which John roughly embraces Rosa.

When Alma tries to prepare her parents for the expected caller, she meets with opposition. Her father, wary of John's reputation for drinking and gambling, tells Alma that she must go upstairs to her room if John comes. Alma defies her parents by going out to meet John. However, she wears not a plume on her hat, but a veil in front of her face.

John takes Alma to Moon Lake Casino. In an arbor with two chairs and a torn paper lantern, they converse and discover their long-standing differences. He lifts her veil to kiss her, but she maintains her ladylike decorum. When he proposes that they go to a room above the casino, she protests and takes a taxi home.

Alma learns from a local busybody that John Buchanan and Rosa Gonzales have taken out a license to be married the next day, an arrangement necessitated by John's debt of several thousand dollars to the casino. Alma telephones the news to the elder Dr. Buchanan, who has been working at the fever clinic in another town. The scene shifts to the doctor's office. There, Rosa dances for John, and he muses: "Did anyone ever slide downhill as fast as I have this summer?" Rosa explains the marriage's importance to her as an escape from squalor. Rosa's father, drunk from the wild party going on in the house, enters and collapses on the couch. John wanders outside alone, drawn to the light in the rectory window. He enters the rectory, kneels beside Alma, and says, "Eternity and Miss Alma have such cool hands." In the doctor's office, Rosa and her father are surprised by the sudden return of Dr. Buchanan. The old doctor strikes out with his cane, and Gonzales reacts by firing his revolver.

Later, while Reverend Winemiller prays over the dying doctor in the next room, John gives Alma an anatomy lecture in which the lines of separation are clearly drawn between them. He confesses, "I'm more afraid of your soul than you're afraid of my body." During the passage of time between this scene and the next, both Alma and John change remarkably. When Alma next appears, she has grown pale and listless, and has refused to leave the rectory except to go for walks in the middle of the night. John, having straightened himself out and completed his father's work at the fever clinic, is welcomed back to town with a band and a parade in his honor. Nellie, now a college girl home for Thanksgiving, cajoles John into kissing her and tells him she will be back for Christmas.

Alma and Nellie meet by the fountain. Nellie gives Alma a Christmas present, a lace handkerchief from her and John. Nellie tells Alma how highly John had spoken of Alma's good influence on him. Alma then goes to visit John in his office; she wears a plumed hat. She has reached her crisis in the play, the point at which she relinquishes her ladylike restraint and offers to meet John on his own terms.

John had previously told Alma that she had a doppelgänger, but only now does the full significance of it become clear. The doppelgänger was the flamelike physical presence of Alma that was constantly drawn to the rectory window facing John's house. Just as Alma was confined in the rectory, her doppelgänger was imprisoned within the icy, spiritual Alma whose very fingers seemed "frozen" when she had tried to unbutton her blouse. Now she tells John that "the girl who said 'no,' she doesn't exist any more, she died last summer—suffocated in smoke from something on fire inside her."

To her dismay, John replies that he has come around to Alma's side of last summer's argument, that although the anatomy chart doesn't indicate much room to spare, "something else is in there, an immaterial something—as thin as smoke." Alma realizes that "the tables have turned with a vengeance." John writes Alma a prescription for the little white pills that calm her fluttering heart. Nellie rushes in to hug Alma, pleased that Alma is the first to know of her engagement to John. Alma fights back her tears and escapes.

In the last scene, Alma drinks from the fountain and takes one of her tablets. She falls into conversation with a novice traveling salesman. He invites her to Moon Lake Casino. Alma goes, perhaps to follow in the footsteps of Nellie's mother, whose reputation was tarnished by her habit of meeting salesmen at the train station. Alma's final gesture is a farewell salute to the angel.

*Eccentricities of a Nightingale* was begun as a revision of *Summer and Smoke* for the 1951 London production. The new version was not used then, and the manuscript was forgotten for many years. It was copyrighted in 1964, but was not produced until 1976.

Williams has said that although the same locale and some of the same characters from *Summer and Smoke* are used in *Eccentricities of a Nightingale*, the latter is a substantially different play, less melodramatic and less conventional. It is also shorter and less complex. The melodrama is obviated by the absence in the new version of Rosa Gonzales, her father, and Moon Lake Casino. Nellie, too, disappears, and John's father is reduced to an offstage presence. One major new character is introduced: Mrs. Buchanan, a dominating mother who coddles and stands guard over her son. John is now a brilliant, self-disciplined young doctor with a promising future. The "less conventional" aspect of the new play may be that Alma's nervous mannerisms have been pushed to the point of eccentricity. Whereas in *Summer and Smoke* Alma behaved conventionally while John ran wild, in the new play Alma is generally considered "odd," and Mrs. Buchanan finds her quite unworthy of John's attention.

Reverend Winemiller and his daughter still have the burden of a mentally aberrant Mrs. Winemiller, but she is treated less as a child than as a social liability. Her frequent references to her sister Albertine suggest that the cause of Mrs. Winemiller's condition is the repression of the sensual side of her nature in her marriage to the minister. Alma finally tells the whole story to her would-be beau Roger Doremus: Alma's Aunt Albertine had also been a minister's daughter, but she ran away from the rectory with a handsome stranger who owned the Musée mécanique in New Orleans. Among its marvels was a mechanical bird-girl from whose mouth a whistling silver bird would fly (this is surely a symbolic counterpart to Alma, whose singing has earned her the nickname "Nightingale of the Delta"). The museum was mortgaged to buy, as an added attraction, a boa constrictor, but when the snake (a Jungian sex symbol) died, they lost everything. Albertine's paramour set fire to the museum. Since Albertine had known her only happiness with him, she ran into the burning building to join him in the consuming flames.

The first and last scenes of *Eccentricities of a Nightingale* occur on the Fourth of July, but most of the action is compressed into the last week of an unusually cold December. On New Year's Eve, John overrides his mother's wishes and takes Alma to the Delta Brilliant to see a Mary Pickford movie. He has told his mother that he is not in love with Miss Alma, but that he respects her "gallantry." After the movie, Alma reveals her love to John and asks him to take her to a rented-by-the-hour hotel room, because she could make a lifetime of such an hour with him. In the cold rented room, John tries to start a fire in the grate. Alma tears the plume from her hat, a frantic sacrifice to feed the dying flame. Like the fire, their relationship has no chance. Church bells ring in the New Year. John kisses Alma and, miraculously, a red glow brightens in the fireplace.

The Epilogue takes place on a Fourth of July night an indefinite time later. In this play Alma is more active in seeking the attention of the traveling salesman, and it is suggested that she has been doing this for some time since her father's death. She has given up singing, which formerly was her only escape from constriction. But now, despite her tarnished reputation, she wears the plume of honesty on her hat as she accompanies the salesman to a rented room.

*Summer and Smoke* was first produced at Theater '47 in Dallas, Texas, under the direction of Margo Jones. It opened July 9, 1947, and played four weeks to capacity houses in the intimate arena-like theater. Miss Jones directed the play again on Broadway in

October 1948. Despite the advantage of a brilliant setting by Jo Mielziner, it was less favorably received in New York. Critics found it vague and somewhat tedious. It fared better in London, where it opened in November 1951 at the small, suburban Lyric Theater. It was moved to the West End's Duchess Theater in January 1952.

In 1950 *Summer and Smoke* was produced by the Actors' Company at the LaJolla Playhouse in California. The cast, led by Dorothy McGuire, John Ireland, and Una Merkel, took the production on a successful fourteen-week railroad tour in the west, performing in college auditoriums and former vaudeville houses. The play had it's second chance in New York when it opened on April 24, 1952, at the intimate Circle in the Square Theater, directed by José Quintero. The production made a star of Geraldine Page and a success of Quintero's theater.

Geraldine Page again played Alma in the 1961 film entitled *Summer and Smoke*. She was supported by Laurence Harvey as John, Una Merkel as Mrs. Winemiller, and Rita Moreno as Rosa Gonzales. An opera version of *Summer and Smoke* by Lee Hoiby was performed at the St. Paul Opera in June 1971 and at the New York City Opera, opening March 19, 1972.

*Eccentricities of a Nightingale* was broadcast on public television, with the collaboration of San Diego's Old Globe Theater Company, on June 16, 1976. Blythe Danner and Frank Langella played Alma and John. This play's Broadway premiere finally came on November 23, 1976. Reactions were mixed. Howard Kissel (*Women's Wear Daily*) wrote: "If the new version is less extravagant, less haunting, it is probably more cogent for contemporary audiences, particularly in the second act, which is a series of solidly, honestly written encounters between the two characters." Referring to the excision of melodramatic elements, Martin Gottfried (*New York Post*) commented: "The worst is gone, but the play is now incomplete."

## 22. *The Rose Tattoo*

"*The Rose Tattoo* was my love-play to the world," Tennessee Williams wrote in his *Memoirs*. His first full-length comedy grew out of the rejuvenating experience of his first visit to Italy and Sicily. The earthiness, warmth, and vitality he found there are transmitted in this humorous modern echo of the ancient Dionysian revels which commemorated nature's cycle of death and rebirth.

The protagonist of Williams's celebration of life is Serafina Delle Rose. At the beginning of the play she is proud to bear the baronial name of her adored husband Rosario Delle Rose. He drives a ten-ton banana truck for a fruit company on the Gulf Coast between New Orleans and Mobile, Alabama. Serafina has a childlike faith in the miraculous, a mixture of religion and superstition. The interior of her house is filled with religious artifacts, including a shrine with a statue of the Madonna, before which a vigil light burns continuously in a ruby cup.

One of Serafina's neighbors in the Sicilian settlement is a woman she calls the Strega, or Witch. Serafina tells her daughter Rosa not to look at the Strega because she has the evil eye. Rosa, more realistic than her mother, knows that the Strega is afflicted with a cataract. Twice during the play, the Strega's black goat gets into Serafina's yard, initiating a comic chase and symbolically underscoring the sexual import of the moment. Serafina's proneness to equate sex with religion is another facet of her simplicity. After she becomes a widow, she tells the priest: "To me the big bed was beautiful like a religion." In the opening scene, she knows that she has conceived because she woke up in the night with a needle-like pain and discovered on her breast, momentarily, the image of her husband's rose tattoo. The rose is the dominant symbol of the play, with its combined religious and sensuous associations. It appears in the pattern of the wallpaper and the carpet, as well as liberally sprinkled throughout Serafina's speech.

Having heard that Serafina does sewing, Estelle Hohengarten, a thin blond woman who is the antithesis of plump, dark Serafina, brings her a length of rose-colored silk to be made into a shirt for the man she loves on the first anniversary of their meeting. Serafina is just completing that job when she learns that her husband has been killed while driving his truck. In her terrible grief, she loses the baby. Despite the objection of her priest, she insists that Rosario's body be cremated and the ashes kept at home in an urn. When Estelle arrives wearing a black veil, the Greek-chorus-like group of neighbor women attacks her and drives her away, to prevent Serafina from learning of her husband's affair with Estelle. It was Estelle who had arranged the contacts for Rosario's dope-smuggling operation, the cause of his death.

Three years later, Serafina's grief has apparently not diminished. She never dresses or goes out, but shuffles about in a stained pink slip. She has become an object of curiosity to the children who play in her yard during much of the action. She has alienated her neighbors and prefers the company of her dressmaker's dummies. Among the mannequins are two, a widow and a bride, whose positions suggest that they are having a violent argument. The bride figure begins to be associated with Rosa, who, at fifteen, has fallen in love with a sailor. Serafina, whether overprotective or unconsciously jealous of her daughter, makes a ridiculous spectacle of herself before she finally allows Rosa to put on her white dress and go to high school graduation.

Serafina hurriedly starts to dress for the graduation but is interrupted by Bessie and Flora, two middle-aged "female clowns," who demand a blouse that was to have been ready. It is in this very comic scene, one of the funniest in the play, that Serafina learns the heart-breaking truth about her husband. In classic farce style, Serafina chases the woman with a broom while the high school band can be heard playing "The Stars and Stripes Forever."

Stunned, but refusing to believe what she has heard, Serafina shuts herself up in the house and begs the Madonna for a "sign." Rosa brings Jack home from graduation to meet her mother. To Rosa's intense embarrassment, Serafina forces Jack to kneel before the Madonna and promise to "respect the innocence of the daughter, Rosa, of Rosario Delle Rose." Rosa and Jack leave for the class picnic before Serafina has a chance to give Rosa her graduation present—a gold wristwatch. Serafina absentmindedly winds up the watch, a sign that time had stopped for her when Rosario died and she can no longer boast as she had in Scene 1: "My clock is my heart and my heart don't say tick-tick, it says love-love!"

Serafina's process of rebirth begins with the arrival of Alvaro Mangiacavallo, a handsome, clownish fellow whose banana truck was forced off the highway near Serafina's house. His day has gone just as badly as hers. He runs into her house to hide his unmanly weeping from the group outside. Their long scene together in Act 2 is "like the meeting of two lonely children." She offers to sew his torn jacket. Startled by the resemblance between his well-built torso and that of her former husband, she pricks herself with the needle. She gives him the pink silk shirt to wear, since it has lain unclaimed in a drawer for three years.

Despite Alvaro's prowess in catching the Strega's black goat, he is too much a buffoon to measure up to her memory of Rosario. Serafina fancies herself the widow of a baron, whereas Alvaro unabashedly admits to being the grandson of a Sicilian village idiot. Yet he does have the compassion to see that Serafina has buried her heart in the urn with the ashes and to tell her that she should let it fly out like a happy bird. Serafina's gradual acceptance of Alvaro with all of his less-than-ideal traits is her coming to terms with reality, despite the fact that reality never measures up to an overblown romantic memory.

Serafina and Alvaro are both very dressed up and nervous when he comes to return the pink shirt to her that evening. His clumsy attempts to seduce her—including the display of a newly acquired rose tattoo on his chest—only repel Serafina. She decides to find out the truth about Rosario. A telephone call confirms that Estelle Hohengarten had indeed had an affair with Rosario and that she even has a rose tattoo on her own breast.

An interesting recurrence of the play's leitmotiv of numbers underlines the buildup of Serafina's extreme emotional reaction to what she has learned. Serafina had earlier told Alvaro: "People are always taking down license numbers and telephone numbers that don't mean nothing—all them numbers . . ." Alvaro had said that his three dependents pass their time playing the numbers. Now, as Serafina recoils dizzily from the telephone, a little boy playing hide-and-seek in the yard counts loudly to one hundred. The order of the numbers is governed by a relentless logic, as relentless as Serafina's irrational passion. She hurls the urn across the room and smashes it, and she blows out the Madonna's vigil light. Having obliterated these two checks on her sensuality—respect for her husband's memory and superstitious religiosity—she says good night to Alvaro loudly enough to be heard by the neighbors, whose curiosity she regards as a third restraint. Then she softly bids Alvaro move his truck and return by the back door.

Just before daybreak, Rosa and Jack return from the picnic. Jack had kept his promise to respect Rosa's innocence, but Rosa insists that she will come to him that afternoon. She wants to go to a hotel with Jack because "they have numbers on doors and sometimes —numbers are—lucky." She enters the house and falls asleep on the sofa.

When the cock crows, Alvaro stumbles sleepily out of the bedroom and sees Rosa. Crouching over her, he exclaims admiringly, "Che bella!," in a voice that echoes the bleats of the goat outside. Rosa awakens and screams. Serafina seizes her broom and chases the half-dressed Alvaro out of the house. She is pathetically funny in her attempt to convince Rosa that she doesn't know how that man got in the house, but Rosa exposes her mother's hypocrisy. Rosa leaves to meet Jack before Serafina can give her the wristwatch. The watch has stopped, an indication to Serafina that she should go back to measuring time by the clock of her heart.

The wind has blown away all the ashes from the smashed urn. From outside Alvaro begins calling for the "happy bird," and the neighbor women make teasing remarks about the man without a shirt. Serafina tosses the rose-colored silk shirt to them, and the women pass it along to Alvaro "like a streak of flame shooting up a dry hill." Serafina, having felt again the burning of the rose on her breast, goes to meet him.

*The Rose Tattoo* opened February 3, 1951, to mixed reviews. While some critics hailed Williams's foray into comedy and his departure from "case histories of neurotic Southern belles," others found the play offensive and even sacrilegious. In the cast were Maureen Stapleton as Serafina, Eli Wallach as Alvaro, Phyllis Love as Rosa, and Don Murray as Jack. Miss Stapleton recreated her role in a revival at the New York City Center that opened on October 20, 1966. After fifteen years, Williams's comic sense was better understood and appreciated.

The 1955 film version was a triumph for Anna Magnani. Her Serafina is larger than life, eloquent in gesture, intonation, and sheer presence. Burt Lancaster pushes Alvaro's buffoonery to extremes. These two performers compensate for a film that is marred by poorly composed shots and bowdlerized dialogue.

## 23. Camino Real

*Camino Real* may be the work that is most expressive of Williams's personal vision, but it is his least typical play, at least of those written before 1962. It stands apart from his other work in its use of archetypical rather than fully developed characters, in its allegorical setting, and in its emphasis on formal technique over narrative content. All of Williams's plays exploit the theatrical value of lighting, music and sound effects, scenic imagery, ritual enactment, and concrete symbols, but *Camino Real* forges them into expressionism.

Expressionism in the arts might be defined as the artist's projection of his own mental states onto external reality, which is thereby transformed. In drama, expressionism may be traced back to *A Dream Play* (1902), through which August Strindberg sought (as he explained in the Preface to that play)

> . . . to reproduce the disconnected but apparently logical form of a dream. Anything can happen; everything is possible and probable. Time and space do not exist; on a slight groundwork of reality, imagination spins and weaves new patterns made up of memories, experiences, unfettered fancies, absurdities, and improvisations.

In his Foreword to the published version of *Camino Real*, Williams stated that his intention was to recreate "the continually dissolving and transforming images of a dream." Most of the dramatic action of *Camino Real* is apparently the dream of Don Quixote, who falls asleep in the Prologue and awakens only toward the end of the final scene. Over all of this, however, is the single consciousness of the artist-dreamer Tennessee Williams, whose personal vocabulary of images forms the substance of the play.

Expressionist plays tend to rely heavily upon scenic effect. Williams wrote in his Afterword to *Camino Real* that of all the works he had written, "this one was meant most for the vulgarity of performance." It employs the episodic construction of expressionist drama in it's formal division into a Prologue and Sixteen Blocks on the Camino Real. Each block is announced by Gutman, "a lordly fat man wearing a linen suit and a pith helmet," from the balcony or terrace of the Siete Mares Hotel. The hotel is built over the locale's only never-dried-up spring, and, according to its proprietor Gutman, that advantage has to be protected sometimes by martial law.

Williams's depiction of Gutman and his police force as exploiters of the ragged populace, as well as of unwary transients, illustrates another facet of expressionism: its social consciousness. The peak of the expressionist movement in the arts was in Germany during and after World War I, when dramatists and filmmakers were concerned about diminishing human values in the face of frighteningly rapid technological progress. The human individual was represented by an everyman-like protagonist. Kilroy in *Camino Real* is such a protagonist, based upon the legendary figure of the ubiquitous American soldier in World War II who would leave his message, "Kilroy was here," one step ahead of everyone else. Kilroy represents the innocent American lost amidst the corruption of older civilizations.

Williams calls for the anglicized pronunciation of the title, *CAmino REal*, to emphasize the very *real* desperation of those who have left the Royal Way (*CaMIno ReAL* in Spanish). The setting is the plaza of a tropical seaport. One side of the stage represents Skid Row, comprised of the Gypsy's stall, the Loan Shark pawnshop, and a fleabag hotel called the Ritz Men Only. The Siete Mares Hotel, opposite, with its outdoor, terraced dining area, represents luxury. Separating the two sides is a flight of steps leading to Tierra Incognita, a vast desolate stretch relieved only by a vista of distant mountains. In the center of the plaza is the dried-up public fountain.

The Prologue occurs just before daybreak. Don Quixote enters down a central aisle of the theater, followed by Sancho Panza. Questing for a rebirth of the

ideals of truth, valor, and *devoir*, Don Quixote advances onto the stage. Sancho realizes that "the spring
of humanity has gone dry in this place," and decides
to retreat. When Gutman's white cockatoo signals the
dawn, Don Quixote falls asleep, mumbling that tomorrow at this same hour he will depart with a new
companion in place of Sancho.

A sun-blackened, ragged man stumbles down the
steps to the fountain. He discovers that it is dry and
moves toward the Siete Mares. Gutman whistles. An
Officer steps forward and shoots this "Survivor" of a
party that had attempted to cross Tierra Incognita.
During the Survivor's extended death throes, some of
the wealthy, decadent hotel guests drift out onto the
terrace. One of them is Jacques Casanova, the famous
seventeenth-century rogue and lover, whose expenses
are now met by Marguerite Gautier, the romantic-era
courtesan, also known as Camille. Casanova's compassionate impulse toward the Survivor is checked by
Gutman's offering him a thimbleful of brandy.

A blind singer, La Madrecita de los Perdidos
(Little Mother of the Lost Ones) goes to the Survivor
and cradles him in her arms in the attitude of a Pietà.
With her is a ragged guitar-player called the Dreamer.
The Dreamer speaks the word that is taboo on the
Camino Real: "Hermano!" (brother). Instantly, the
starving street people begin to riot, "for what is a
brother to them," says Gutman, "but someone to get
ahead of, to cheat, to lie to, to undersell in the
market." As a diversion Gutman calls for a fiesta. The
Gypsy announces that at tonight's fiesta the moon
will restore the virginity of her daughter Esmeralda.
With the people distracted by a dance, Guards force
La Madrecita and the Dreamer to abandon the lifeless
body of the Survivor.

Kilroy enters. He has a pair of golden boxing gloves hanging about his neck and a gem-studded belt with the word "Champ." He explains to an Officer that he became a vagrant because of his defective heart—"a heart in my chest as big as the head of a baby"— which forced his retirement from the prize ring. Kilroy asks where this place is, but the Officer brutally elbows him aside. Kilroy's pocket is picked. He watches the Streetcleaners arrive and stuff the body of the Survivor into their white barrel. Hungry and destitute, he enters the Loan Shark's shop to hock his "sweet used-to-be," the Champ's belt.

Kilroy's next encounter is with the Baron de Charlus, a sophisticated degenerate from Marcel Proust's novel *Remembrance of Things Past.* The Baron falls prey to the Streetcleaners, and Kilroy turns to Casanova for information. He learns that those whose pockets are empty when picked up by the Street-cleaners are taken to the Laboratory, where their chemical components are "collectivized," with the profits going to support the police. The only escape route from Camino Real is across Tierra Incognita. Neither Kilroy nor Casanova is quite ready to attempt that yet.

Since Kilroy is unemployed and can produce no witness to the fact that he was robbed, Gutman forces him to become the Patsy—the one who takes all the pratfalls for his superiors. Kilroy runs from the Officers who have brought him the clown costume, at the same time as Esmeralda escapes from the Gypsy's stall and is pursued by her brother Abdallah and by Nursie. The two chase sequences occur simultaneously, and both end in defeat for the pursued. The Gypsy slaps Esmeralda and drags her away. Kilroy is dressed in a clown suit with a nose that lights up when he presses a button.

Marguerite Gautier returns to the Siete Mares from an afternoon of drugs and paid lovers at Ahmed's. She has been robbed of her passport and residence permit. She and Casanova take their usual table on the terrace, but a screen is placed around them, since Lord and Lady Mulligan object to the presence of such people. Casanova tells her that he has learned of another way to leave the Camino Real—a nonscheduled flight called the Fugitivo. As long as they are together like caged birds, Casanova offers Marguerite his love "until the time or way comes that we both can leave with honor." She replies:

> Leave with honor? Your vocabulary is almost as out-of-date as your cape and your cane. How could anyone quit this field with honor, this place where there's nothing but the gradual wasting away of everything decent in us . . . the sort of desperation that comes after desperation has been worn out through long wear!

Lord Byron enters and announces his departure, "the furthest departure a man could make," a departure from his present self to the self he used to be. He recalls the cremation of his fellow poet Shelley and how Shelley's friend Trelawney had snatched the heart out of the burning corpse. He asks what one man can do with another's heart. Casanova answers by demonstrating with a loaf of bread; the heart can be twisted, torn, crushed, and kicked away. Lord Byron replies that a poet's vocation is "to influence the heart in a gentler fashion, . . . to purify it and lift it above its ordinary level. For what is the heart but a sort of—a sort of—*instrument*!—that translates noise into music, chaos into—order . . .—*a mysterious order*!" This sequence is clearly the "heart" of the play, set (in Block

Eight) exactly midway through the action, and most directly stating Williams's own beliefs. Lord Byron's sense of loss—the feeling that his vocation has been "obscured by vulgar plaudits"—recalls the sentiment Williams expressed in his essay "The Catastrophe of Success" (published as a Preface to *The Glass Menagerie*). Lord Byron sets out to cross Tierra Incognita.

The sound of the Fugitivo is heard, and guests at the Siete Mares begin scrambling to collect their possessions and pass customs inspection. Marguerite sends Casanova to get her money from the hotel safe, and she frantically tries to wrangle a ticket. Without her papers, she misses the Fugitivo. Consolingly, Casanova again offers his love, but Marguerite says that it is only familiarity that passes for love on the Camino Real. Tenderness is like delicate violets that somehow can grow on the moon or in the mountains, but that cannot break the rocks. Flaunting Casanova, Marguerite arranges to spend the night at Ahmed's.

The Fiesta begins with Casanova's being crowned with gilded antlers as King of Cuckolds. While the crowd's attention is focussed on the rising of the moon, which heralds the restoration of Esmeralda's virginity, Kilroy and Casanova embrace as brothers. They help each other to remove the antlers and the clown suit. Kilroy decides to pawn his golden gloves to finance his trip across Tierra Incognita. He reemerges from the Loan Shark in disguise, only to find that he has become Esmeralda's Chosen Hero.

The Gypsy fills out the forms for the Chosen Hero and incidentally informs Kilroy that the Streetcleaners are waiting for him. She takes the ten dollars Kilroy got for his golden gloves and leaves him with Esmeralda. Kilroy finally convinces Esmeralda that he is sincere. She allows him to lift her veil, but he is immediately filled with disappointment and regret. Kilroy leaves the Gypsy's establishment and, hoping to evade the Streetcleaners, pleads with Gutman for admission to the Siete Mares. Meanwhile, Casanova is evicted. His suitcase full of fragile mementos is tossed from the balcony. He invites Kilroy to share a room at the Ritz Men Only, but Kilroy declines.

Marguerite enters with an escort who suddenly snatches her purse and necklace and frisks her degradingly, then runs off. Kilroy hears the Streetcleaners coming. He tells Marguerite to get inside quickly, but she stays, holding his hand. Kilroy goes down fighting.

In Block Fifteen, La Madrecita holds Kilroy's lifeless body across her knees, saying, "This was thy son, America—and now mine." At the same time a Medical Instructor describes Kilroy to his students while referring to a sheeted body on the dissecting table. The Instructor opens the corpse's chest cavity and removes a pure gold heart as big as the head of a baby. The ghost of Kilroy rises from La Madrecita's lap, grabs his heart from the Instructor, and dashes confusedly about the theater to the sound of wailing sirens, whistles, motors, screeching brakes, pistol shots, and thundering footsteps. Esmeralda appears on the roof of the Gypsy's establishment. She wears a child's nightgown. She kneels to say her bedtime prayer:

> God bless all con men and hustlers and pitch-men who hawk their hearts on the street, all two-time losers who're likely to lose once more, the courtesan who made the mistake of love, the greatest of lovers crowned with the longest horns, the poet who wandered far from his heart's green country and possibly will and possibly won't be able to find his way back, look down with a smile tonight on the last cavaliers, the ones with the rusty armor and soiled white plumes, and visit with understanding and something that's almost

tender those fading legends that come and go in
this plaza like songs not clearly remembered, oh,
sometime and somewhere, let there be something
to mean the word *honor* again!

Kilroy decides to go to Esmeralda again as the Chosen
Hero. He pawns his gold heart to buy presents for
her, but is repulsed—"baptised with the contents of a
slop jar."

Don Quixote wakes up. He goes to the fountain,
which begins to flow. He tells Kilroy not to pity himself and invites him to join him in crossing Tierra
Incognita. Marguerite comes out onto the terrace and
sends a message to Casanova at the Ritz Men Only:
she will guarantee his tabs at the Siete Mares and expects him to join her for breakfast. Their reconciliation may be permanent this time, for at the top of
the stairs Don Quixote announces: "The violets in the
mountains have broken the rocks!"

An early version of the play, entitled *Ten Blocks
on the Camino Real*, was finished early in 1946. Williams sent it to Audrey Wood, his agent, who told
him, according to one of Williams's letters to Donald
Windham, that the best scene was "too coarse." In
*Memoirs*, Williams recalls that she told him to "put
it away" and "not let anybody see it." That "medium-
length play" is included in the acting edition of
*American Blues*.

*Camino Real* was considered a failure in its Broadway premiere on March 19, 1953. Most critics wrote
that the play's significance was beyond their compre-
hension or else that it was hyperbole without significance. Only William Hawkins of the *New York
World-Telegram* was entirely favorable toward the
"brilliant and riotous adventure" which, he said,

"succeeds in making tangible for all your senses the delirious pains and ecstasy of a wild dream."

Nor was the play well received by critics of productions in Bochum, Germany, in March 1955, or in London in April 1957. José Quintero's Circle in the Square revival in May 1960 at the St. Mark's Theater was hampered by the poor acoustics of that theater, combined with "slovenly speaking by actors who have no dimension beyond naturalism" (Brooks Atkinson, *New York Times*).

Seventeen years after its original production, Williams's "ode to losers" drew much praise from Broadway critics. This revival, directed by Milton Katselas and starring Al Pacino as Kilroy, had originally been staged at the Mark Taper Forum in Los Angeles. It opened at the Vivian Beaumont Theater, Lincoln Center, on January 8, 1970. Clive Barnes observed that "our standards of obscurity, like our standards of obscenity, have escalated," and that although *Camino Real* still sounded "a little fuddled, a little punch drunk," it might be Williams's best play.

## 24. Cat on a Hot Tin Roof

Like so many others of Williams's full-length plays, *Cat on a Hot Tin Roof* has undergone several metamorphoses. It began as a short story, "Three Players of a Summer Game," in 1952 (published in *Hard Candy*). The only characters transferred from the story to the play are Brick Pollitt, formerly a celebrated college athlete who now has a drinking problem, and his wife Margaret. After the 1955 New York production of the play, *Cat on a Hot Tin Roof* was always published with two different versions of Act 3, accompanied by Williams's "Note of Explanation." The first Act 3 was Williams's original and preferred version. The second, or Broadway, version incorporated changes suggested by director Elia Kazan, whose theatrical acumen Williams deeply respected.

Kazan had asked that Big Daddy be brought back onstage in Act 3, since he was too vivid and important a character to disappear after the second-act curtain; that some transformation be effected in Brick's character as a result of his confrontation with Big Daddy in Act 2; and that Margaret be made more clearly sympathetic to the audience. The original Act 3 allows the actor playing Big Daddy to build to a much stronger emotional climax at the end of Act 2, but the Broadway version has the advantage of enabling Maggie to tell her crucial lie to Big Daddy's face.

For the 1974 American Shakespeare Theater production, Williams again rewrote Act 3 and made a number of other revisions throughout the play's text. This last, and presumably definitive, version retains Big Daddy's appearance and Maggie's enhanced sympathetic qualities, but reverts to the original treatment of Brick, which Williams had explained as follows:

> I felt that the moral paralysis of Brick was a root thing in his tragedy, and to show a dramatic progression would obscure the meaning of that tragedy in him and because I don't believe that a conversation, however revelatory, ever effects so immediate a change in the heart or even conduct of a person in Brick's state of spiritual disrepair.

It is this version that will be examined here.

The tight classical structure of the play—its action confined in space to a single setting and in time to the actual duration of the performance—emphasizes the magnitude of the human concerns that clash so violently within this framework. In a bed-sitting-room of a Mississippi Delta plantation home, characters grope toward one another and attempt to communicate across opposing currents of lies and truth, which ironically underscore the opposing forces of life and death. The constant discordant interplay of personalities and drives in this room contrasts with the muted, poetic quality of the setting. The room has two pairs of wide doors opening onto an upstairs gallery, through which the visible sky changes during the course of the play from summer afternoon sunlight to dusk and to night.

Act 1 is a *tour de force* for the actress playing Margaret, or, as she calls herself, Maggie the Cat. She enters the bedroom she occupies with her husband Brick Pollitt and begins a virtually act-long monologue, punctuated at intervals by snatches of dialogue with Brick and by three brief visits by others to their room. Brick is confined to the room because he had broken his ankle the night before when he was drunkenly jumping hurdles at 3:00 A.M. on the high school athletic field, a scene of his past glories. Maggie has left the dinner table in order to change clothes, because one of Mae and Gooper's children hit her with a hot buttered biscuit. Maggie tells Brick that his brother Gooper, a lawyer, is planning to cut him out of the estate, since their father, Big Daddy Pollitt, is dying of cancer and has made no will. Big Daddy and Big Mama have been lulled by a false report from the Ochsner Clinic that Big Daddy has only a small functional disorder.

Having come from a socially respectable but poverty-stricken background, Maggie is determined that she and Brick inherit Big Daddy's estate. Her determination is impeded by the fact that Brick has left his job as a nationally known sports announcer and taken to drink, and that she and Brick are childless, while Mae and Gooper have five children, with a sixth on the way. Maggie's most serious problem is her loneliness: she loves Brick, but, for reasons that are gradually revealed, he cannot stand her. He has, however, agreed, in his cool, detached manner, to continue living with her.

Sounds of croquet on the lawn below—the click of mallets and light voices—are heard in counterpoint to Maggie's pleas for affection. The croquet game, Brick's former athleticism, and the calculated strategies of Mae and Gooper provide a vocabulary of gamesmanship throughout the play. Maggie tells Brick:

> Of course you always had that detached quality as if you were playing a game without much concern over whether you won or lost, and now that you've lost the game, not lost but just quit playing, you have that rare sort of charm that usually only happens in very old or hopelessly sick people, the charm of the defeated.

Mae brings in a bow from a lady's archery set and tells Maggie that she shouldn't leave such things about in a house full of "nawmal rid-blooded children attracted t' weapons." Their very short exchange establishes "Sister Woman" Mae as a gushing, ridiculous "mom," who brings out the "catty" side of Maggie. When Mae leaves, Maggie asks herself, "WHY!—Am I so catty?—Cause I'm consumed with envy an' eaten up with longing?"

When Big Mama comes to the room, Bricks shuts himself in the bathroom. A short, stout woman of sixty wearing "at least half a million in flashy gems," Big Mama is elated by the clinic report on Big Daddy's condition. Changing to the subject of Brick, she implicates Maggie as the cause of her favorite son's drinking problem. She exits, leaving Maggie feeling more alone than ever.

Maggie tries to awaken in Brick some attraction to her, but instead gets caught up in the recollection of what went wrong between them. Their marriage was blissfully happy at first. After graduation they and Brick's best friend Skipper went on the road with the Dixie Stars. Skipper began drinking heavily, and Maggie suspected it was because Skipper was homosexually attracted to Brick. She tried to get Skipper to face the truth by coming to his hotel room one night while Brick was hospitalized with an injury. "Skipper and I made love," she says, "if love you could call it, because it made both of us feel a little bit closer to you."

Maggie says that she cannot whitewash her own behavior, but that she does deserve credit for her honesty. Brick strikes at her with his crutch. She insists, "Skipper is dead! I'm alive! Maggie the cat is— alive!" He throws his crutch at her and falls to the floor. One of Mae's children bursts into the room shooting a cap pistol and jeering at Maggie. The act ends with the whole family on their way up to Brick's room for Big Daddy's birthday party.

Act 2 begins with the entrance of Big Daddy, followed by Reverend Tooker, Gooper, Mae, Dr. Baugh, and Big Mama. Big Mama scolds Brick for his drinking, as he drains another glass. Servants bring in a cake and champagne. Mae directs her children in a song to Big Daddy. Big Daddy cuts short the hypocritical jockeying for his favor and tries to question

Brick about his broken ankle. It is readily apparent what Williams meant when he wrote in *Memoirs* that he had given Big Daddy "a kind of crude eloquence of expression . . . that I have managed to give to no other character of my creation."

When Big Daddy bellows furiously in response to a sixty-fifth birthday toast, everyone except Big Mama slips out onto the gallery. Big Daddy says, "I put up with a whole lot of crap around here because I thought I was dying." But now he refuses to put up with any more lies and liars, including the hypocrisy of his forty-year marriage to Big Mama. She protests that she has always loved him: "I even loved your hate and your hardness, Big Daddy!" She sobs and runs out to the gallery. He muses, "Wouldn't it be funny if that was true. . . ."

Big Daddy calls for Brick. The rest of the act is a long, skillfully constructed confrontation between the two, punctuated with brief intrusions by Big Mama and Reverend Tooker and by Gooper's and Mae's attempts to eavesdrop. Big Daddy reveals that he is not blind to the way the wives are "squaring off" on his land. He is disgusted by Mae's eavesdropping on Brick and Maggie at night and then reporting to Big Mama that Brick refuses to sleep with Maggie. He ruminates on the extent of his wealth and possessions, including "twenty-eight thousand acres of the richest land this side of the valley Nile," and reluctantly concludes that a man cannot buy his life. Now that he is relieved of his fear of imminent death, Big Daddy wants to talk; but Brick wants only to be left in peace with his drink.

Big Daddy finally turns from his own preoccupations to interrogate Brick about his drinking: "Now that I'm straightened out, I'm going to straighten out you! . . . Why are you throwing your life away, boy, like somethin' disgusting you picked up on the street?" Brick replies that he drinks out of "disgust," and, further pressed, says he is disgusted with "mendacity." Big Daddy knows all about mendacity; he has accepted it by living with his "pretenses" toward Big Mama, Gooper, "Mae and those five same screechers out there," "the fool preacher," "Clubs!—Elks! Masons! Rotary!—*crap!*" He does like Brick for some reason, but he does not want to turn his property over to an alcoholic. Now that the pressure is gone, he can wait and see if Brick pulls himself together.

A fireworks display outside the window underlines the emotional intensity of the rest of the act. Big Daddy returns to the subject of Brick's drinking, which started when his friend Skipper died. Brick becomes fiercely defensive. He says, "Skipper and me had a clean, true thing between us! . . . Normal? No!—It was too rare to be normal, any true thing between two people is too rare to be normal." Brick repeats the story Maggie told in Act 1, but Big Daddy presses him for the rest of the story. Brick admits that he received a long-distance telephone call from Skipper, "in which he made a drunken confession to me and on which I hung up!" Big Daddy accuses Brick of killing his friend by not facing the truth with him. Brick turns the tables by telling Big Daddy the truth about his condition: "How about these birthday congratulations, these many, many happy returns of the day, when ev'rybody knows there won't be any except you!" Big Daddy's reaction builds to a tremendous peak. Then he exits, and the act ends.

The family gathers in the room again in Act 3. Mae asks the preacher to stay and be with them when Dr. Baugh tells Big Mama "the actual truth" about the report from the clinic. The group surrounds Big Mama, while Mae and Gooper drop macabre hints about Big Daddy. When the truth is finally revealed, Big Mama calls for Brick, who remains detached from the scene. Reverend Tooker and Dr. Baugh slip away. Mae brings Gooper his briefcase, and he starts to overwhelm Big Mama with paperwork and plans for running the estate. The storm that builds inside the room is echoed by a thunderstorm outside. Big Mama finally rises to the occasion and borrows Big Daddy's word to show her disgust with Gooper's "plans": "CRAP!"

Big Daddy enters, as Gooper hastily stuffs papers back into his briefcase. Big Daddy's attitude is now quite Olympian. He tells an obscene story to make the point that he has noticed "a powerful and obnoxious odor of mendacity in this room." Maggie says she has another birthday present for Big Daddy. She kneels before him and tells him that she and Brick have conceived a child. Big Daddy accepts Maggie's lie, and says he will see his lawyer in the morning. He exits, with Big Mama following. Mae tries to discredit Maggie, but Brick turns on the phonograph to cut her off. Mae and Gooper exit.

Brick says that he has finally drunk enough to get the click in his head that makes him peaceful. He pours another drink and goes out onto the gallery. Maggie gathers all the bottles from the liquor cabinet and takes them out of the room. When she and Brick have both reentered, she tells him that it is her time by the calendar to conceive, and that, after they have made the lie come true, she will bring back the liquor and they will get drunk together. To her declaration of love, Brick muses: "Wouldn't it be funny if that was true?"

"*Cat on a Hot Tin Roof* is a beautifully written, perfectly directed, stunningly acted play of evasions," wrote Walter Kerr (*New York Herald Tribune*) of the production that opened March 24, 1955. Other critics were similarly impressed by the play, Kazan's direction, Jo Mielziner's setting, and the performances of Barbara Bel Geddes as Maggie, Burl Ives as Big Daddy, Ben Gazzara as Brick, and Mildred Dunnock as Big Mama. Richard Watts, Jr. (*New York Post*) wrote: "It is, I think, the final paradox of the work that it is insistently vulgar, morbid, neurotic, and ugly and still maintains a quality of exotic lyricism." This response to what became Williams's longest-running play was a fitting tribute on the tenth anniversary of his Broadway debut.

Burl Ives repeated the role of Big Daddy in the 1958 film version, which also features Elizabeth Taylor as Maggie and Paul Newman as Brick. Richard Brooks directed the generally skillful adaptation of the play, hampered mainly by the screenplay's need to obscure the references to homosexuality.

When the American Shakespeare Theater production was brought to New York on September 24, 1974, Clive Barnes wrote in the *New York Times*: "People used to think that Tennessee Williams's plays were about sex and violence. How wrong they were—they are about love and survival." The consensus was that the production belonged to Elizabeth Ashley as Maggie. She was supported by Keir Dullea as Brick, Fred Gwynne as Big Daddy, and Kate Reid as Big Mama. The production was directed by Michael Kahn.

An NBC-TV production of *Cat on a Hot Tin Roof*, broadcast December 6, 1976, featured Natalie Wood, Robert Wagner, Laurence Olivier, and Maureen Stapleton in the major roles.

## 25. Baby Doll

Williams's first original screenplay, *Baby Doll* (1956), was based upon two of his one-act plays written about ten years earlier. The basic situation and motivations in the film are taken from *27 Wagons Full of Cotton.* An additional character, Aunt Rose, and the first names of the husband and wife characters were provided by *The Long Stay Cut Short; or, The Unsatisfactory Supper.* The film was shot on location in rural Mississippi, the setting of the two short plays.

Archie Lee Meighan is an unpleasant, perpetually sweating, vulgar old man, owner of a cotton gin that is verging on bankruptcy, since the nearby Syndicate Plantation and Gin has taken over all of the business around Tiger Tail Bayou. He and his wife Baby Doll are living under an agreement made with her father shortly before his death. Archie Lee agreed to provide all material comforts for Baby Doll and to let her sleep alone in her crib until her twentieth birthday.

Only two days before Baby Doll's twentieth birthday, the Ideal Pay as You Go Plan Furniture Company repossesses its five complete rooms of furniture, leaving the once-elegant large old house, now filthy and rotting, virtually bare except for Baby Doll's crib and Aunt Rose Comfort's piano. Baby Doll, whose education extended only through fourth grade, threatens to get a job and move to the Kotton King Hotel in town, since Archie Lee can no longer provide for her.

Baby Doll's Aunt Rose Comfort is another source of irritation to Archie Lee. The senile old woman cooks for the Meighans, cuts roses—she calls them "poems of nature"—for the house even after the furniture is gone, and sings hymns. The kind of opposition that was created between Blanche DuBois and Stanley Kowalski in *A Streetcar Named Desire*, that of the finer instincts against the animal ones, is repeated in a minor mode between Aunt Rose Comfort and Archie Lee. Aunt Rose also generates a large share of the comedy in *Baby Doll*. She screams every time the telephone rings. Whenever people she knows are registered at the county hospital, Aunt Rose Comfort goes to call on them and to eat up their chocolate candy.

Silva Vacarro is introduced into the film at a party celebrating his first anniversary as superintendent of the Syndicate Plantation and Gin. He is a dark, handsome young Italian who habitually carries a leather whip. A fire breaks out in the Syndicate Gin, and Vacarro is the only one able to stretch the water hose all the way to the flames. He walks into the burning building and returns with a gasoline can as evidence of arson. By associating Vacarro with his often-used symbols of fire and water, Williams suggests that this outsider among the Southern-rural folk represents purity and energy in a corrupt, decadent milieu.

Rightly suspecting Archie Lee as the arsonist, Vacarro the next day brings his twenty-seven wagons full of cotton to be ginned by him. Archie Lee tells Baby Doll to entertain Mr. Vacarro while he goes to work. Vacarro gets a cool drink of water from the old-fashioned hand pump in the yard. Baby Doll later tells him, "you're the first person could draw it." During the long, hot day, Vacarro begins a gradual, calculated seduction of Baby Doll and, playing upon her fear of ghosts in the old house during a childlike game of hide-and-seek, gets her to sign a statement attesting that Archie Lee set fire to the Syndicate Gin.

That evening, when Aunt Rose serves her "unsatisfactory supper" of undercooked greens, Baby Doll is a changed person. She seems to have matured. Archie

Lee expects that at midnight she will become his wife in more than name only, but Baby Doll now holds the threat of testifying that he committed arson. While Archie Lee is on the telephone, she embraces Vacarro and tells him to leave until Archie Lee calms down.

Baby Doll and Aunt Rose Comfort begin packing to move out. (Vacarro has invited Aunt Rose to come and cook for him.) Archie Lee grabs a shotgun and searches outside the house for Vacarro, firing at random. Baby Doll calls the police, identifying herself as "the ex-Mrs. Meighan." Meanwhile, Vacarro has hidden in the branches of a tree, where Baby Doll manages to join him, unseen by Archie Lee. The police arrive and take Archie Lee away. The published screenplay, which varies somewhat from the film, ends with Vacarro helping Baby Doll down from the tree into his arms, while Aunt Rose Comfort sings "Rock of Ages."

The cast of *Baby Doll* included Carroll Baker as Baby Doll, Karl Malden as Archie Lee, Eli Wallach as Silva Vacarro, and Mildred Dunnock as Aunt Rose Comfort. The latter three discuss the making of the film in interviews with Mike Steen in *A Look at Tennessee Williams*. Elia Kazan's direction of the film tended to emphasize the more degenerate implications of the script. Released in 1956, *Baby Doll* was widely criticized as obscene and immoral, and it did not do well at the box office. Ironically, Williams had intended it as a comedy. Given the opportunity to see the film again after an interval of several years, Williams declared the film to be among the very best ever made of his work. He still finds it very funny and innocent. Perhaps it will be appreciated in that vein when Williams releases his stage version entitled *Tiger Tail*.

## 26. Suddenly Last Summer

In *Suddenly Last Summer*, Williams employs a technique used in Sophocles' *Oedipus Rex*. The protagonist compulsively uncovers information about the past, bit by bit, which will seal his or her fate in the present. Both plays employ more narrative than dramatic action to create a steadily mounting sense of horror. Both plays are masterpieces of compression. The running time of *Suddenly Last Summer* is less than an hour and a half.

Williams's setting creates a Southern Gothic atmosphere; it is the fantastic tropical garden of a mansion in the Garden District of New Orleans:

> There are massive tree-flowers that suggest organs of a body, torn out, still glistening with undried blood; there are harsh cries and sibilant hissings and thrashing sounds in the garden as if it were inhabited by beasts, serpents and birds, all of savage nature. . . .

The play's dominant image, that of the predator, is established immediately when Mrs. Venable, the lady of the house, shows Dr. Cukrowicz the garden that had belonged to her son Sebastian and which includes an insectivorous Venus's-flytrap. She also tells the doctor about a visit to the Encantadas Islands she and her son had made one summer. They had watched new-hatched sea turtles make their dash for the sea under attack from a sky full of carnivorous birds that dived down and flipped over the turtles to expose their soft undersides, and ate the flesh. In that terrible scene, Sebastian believed he had seen the image of God.

Mrs. Venable talks at length about her son Sebastian, who had traveled with his mother for twenty-five summers, producing each year a single poem to be read by no one but her. The previous summer Sebastian had traveled with his cousin Catharine instead of his mother, and he had died on that trip without writing his poem. Now Mrs. Venable wants Dr. Cukrowicz to perform a prefrontal lobotomy on Catharine to prevent her from repeating her outrageous story about what happened to Sebastian. In return, Mrs. Venable will set up a sizeable endowment fund to support Dr. Cukrowicz's badly underbudgeted facilities and research program in brain surgery.

Mrs. Venable and the doctor go into the house. Catharine, who has been confined at St. Mary's asylum, is brought to the garden by a white-clad nun. She is reunited with her mother and her brother George, who quickly reveal their grotesquely predatory natures. George wears Sebastian's clothes, which he has inherited, but Mrs. Holly and her son fear that if Catharine continues to repeat her nightmarish story, they will lose the hundred thousand dollars tied up in probate that Sebastian had bequeathed to them.

Returning to the garden, Mrs. Venable squabbles with the detested relatives of her deceased husband, while Dr. Cukrowicz watches passively. Catharine is given an injection and she begins, slowly at first, with interruptions from her listeners, to tell her story. Catharine loved Sebastian because he was kind to her, but she eventually realized that he was a homosexual and was using her to make contacts for him. He had used his mother in the same way without Mrs. Venable's realizing it, until she had a stroke which partially disfigured her. Catharine and Sebastian had gone to Cabeza de Lobo, and there Sebastian gathered a following of homeless, hungry young people whom he exploited.

Catharine's story gathers momentum as she relates how, one blazing hot white day, she and Sebastian were eating lunch at an open-air restaurant when a group of thin, naked, dark-skinned children assembled nearby, cried out for bread, and serenaded them with musical instruments made out of tin cans. Leaving the restaurant, she and Sebastian began to walk uphill in the street. The band followed them. Sebastian started to run. The children screamed and ran to overtake him. Catharine ran back down hill to get help. When she and the police found Sebastian, he was lying naked in the street, cannibalized: the children had cut at him with their jagged tin cans and devoured parts of him.

Mrs. Venable screams, "State asylum, cut this hideous story out of her brain!" The play ends with Dr. Cukrowicz's reaction: "I think we ought at least to consider the possibility that the girl's story could be true. . . ."

*Suddenly Last Summer* has been called a morality play, that is, a dramatized allegory of struggle between forces of good and evil. Dr. Cukrowicz must choose between Catharine, the only character in the play whose primary impulse has always been to love, and Mrs. Venable, who is willing to buy his cooperation. Sebastian, faced with a similar struggle in his social interactions, was punished for his limited, self-contained vision of a world whose natural order is cruelty. Having planned and designed everything in his life, having carved out each day like a piece of sculpture, the poet completed his image of himself as a sacrifice to a terrible God. Part of the theatricality of the play lies in its use of a double frame of reference, first the tropical jungle world of Mrs. Venable, then the realm of Catharine's memory. Catharine's story may be incredibly shocking, but it gains credence by juxtaposition with the fact that sane and civilized characters are prepared to go to such a horrible extreme to quiet her.

*Suddenly Last Summer* was first produced on a bill with Williams's one-act *Something Unspoken*. The joint title for the production, *Garden District*, refers to the fashionable area of uptown New Orleans where the Anglo-American gentry of the pre-Civil War period built their lavish mansions surrounded by gardens. The production opened January 7, 1958, under the direction of Herbert Machiz, who had chosen the play for Anne Meacham as Catharine. Brooks Atkinson (*New York Times*, January 8 and 19, 1958) praised the setting, the direction, the performances, and, above all, Williams's "genius with the language. Although his world is tainted with corruption, it is beautifully contrived. No one else can use ordinary words with so much grace, allusiveness, sorcery, and power."

London theater critics were more restrained in their reaction to the production that opened there on September 16, 1958. The first Paris production of *Suddenly Last Summer*, in 1965, was more favorably received than Williams's earlier plays had been. French critics, who had complained of the brutality and unhealthy sensuality in such plays as *A Streetcar Named Desire*, *Cat on a Hot Tin Roof*, and *Orpheus Descending*, finally perceived Williams's poetic use of language and atmosphere.

The 1959 film version is weakened by the substitution of flashback scenes for Catharine's simple narration. But Dr. Cukrowicz's moral dilemma is intensified by a dramatization of the primitive conditions under which he must perform his delicate work, by the desire of his superior at the clinic to accept Mrs. Venable's gift on her terms, and by the development of romantic interest between Cukrowicz and Catharine. The latter two roles were played by Montgomery Clift and Elizabeth Taylor; Katharine Hepburn played Mrs. Venable. The film was directed by Joseph L. Mankiewicz.

## 27. Sweet Bird of Youth

Two of Williams's major themes predominate in *Sweet Bird of Youth*: the corrupting effects of time and the desire to recapture lost purity. The chief exponents of these preoccupations are two unlikely companions thrown together at a time of crisis in both their lives. Alexandra Del Lago is an aging actress fleeing from what she perceives to be a disastrous, humiliating movie comeback. Her companion is Chance Wayne, a handsome young man with thinning blond hair, whom she picked up in Palm Beach, where he was working as a beach boy.

When the play opens, they are together in a bedroom of the Royal Palms Hotel in St. Cloud, Mississippi. Chance has brought Miss Del Lago, traveling as Princess Kosmonopolis, to his hometown. He plans to blackmail her into launching him and his hometown girlfriend, Heavenly Finley, into movie careers.

While Alexandra is still asleep, Chance receives a visit from George Scudder, the young chief of staff at the local hospital. Scudder says that Chance's mother had been buried at the local church's expense two weeks previously, since Chance could not be reached. Scudder also warns Chance not to try to contact Heavenly, but to leave town immediately.

Alexandra awakens and does not remember who

Chance is or where she is. She calls for a pink pill, vodka, and her oxygen inhalator, all of which Chance supplies. Then he switches on a hidden tape recorder and engages her in conversation, leading her on until she mentions her name and the fact that she carries hashish. She prefers, however, to talk about her plight as an aging artist: "There's nowhere else to retire to when you retire from an art. . . . You can't retire with the outcrying heart of an artist still crying out, in your body, in your nerves, in your what? Heart?" Her desperation is underscored by a recurring musical theme called "The Lament," which blends with the sound of the wind through the tall palm trees outside. A periodic rush of gulls flying past the window, seen as "shadows sweeping the blind," suggests the fleeting passage of time.

Alexandra Del Lago is not intimidated by the threat of blackmail. She frequently refers to herself as a "monster" and she knows how to keep Chance in his place. When, in Scene 2, she signs a number of traveler's checks for Chance, it is explicity in payment for love-making. She asks Chance to tell her his life story as a kind of audition or screen test; if it holds her interest, she will have her studio hire him. Chance recalls his charmed youth in St. Cloud, when his good looks and ambition set him apart from his contemporaries. He went to New York, sang in the chorus of *Oklahoma!*, and pursued his "other vocation . . . love-making," living off "millionaires' widows and wives and debutante daughters." Periodically, he returned to St. Cloud to impress the townspeople and to see Heavenly. He had been Heavenly's lover since he was seventeen, but was prevented from marrying her by her father, politician Boss Finley. Now his "chance" has "waned," and the townspeople consider him a loser.

Alexandra is drawn to Chance. She sees him as "a lost little boy that I really would like to help find himself." She allows him to take her Cadillac convertible with big silver horns. Then, wearing the fine clothes she has bought him and flashing a wad of money, he can drive around town and show off.

Act 2 opens on the terrace of Boss Finley's house. Boss, his son Tom Junior, and Scudder are determined to get rid of Chance, by violence if necessary. Tom Junior reveals himself to be a worthless profligate who is both used and protected by his powerful father. Boss's demeanor softens when he is alone with his beautiful daughter Heavenly. But he orders her to put on a white dress and accompany him that evening to sit on the platform at his political rally in the Royal Palms Hotel. He hopes this will squelch the rumors that have been provoked by a heckler whenever Boss Finley has spoken on "the threat of desegregation to women's chastity in the South."

Heavenly refuses to take part in such a charade. The heckler's jibes are true: Heavenly is sterile as a result of an operation performed on her by Scudder. She regrets both her own and Chance's lost youthful purity: "Papa, there was a time when you could have saved me, by letting me marry a boy that was still young and clean, but instead you drove him away, drove him out of St. Cloud." Boss tells Heavenly that Chance is back in St. Cloud and that, unless she goes to the rally, there will be "consequences" for him that she won't like. It becomes clear that these "consequences" would be the same as those inflicted by Finley's men upon a young black man found on a street after midnight: castration. Boss leaves to pay his daily call on Miss Lucy, his mistress, at the Royal Palms.

The second scene of Act 2 is set in the hotel's cocktail lounge. Miss Lucy recognizes the heckler, gives him a newspaper to hide his face until Boss Finley starts to speak, and wishes him more luck than he is likely to have. Chance enters and tries to show off his sophistication for the hometown couples in the bar, but they snub him. Heavenly's sweet-spirited Aunt Nonnie comes to warn Chance to leave, and Miss Lucy offers to take him to the airport. But Chance stead-fastly proclaims that he intends to take Heavenly away and make her a star through the patronage of his traveling companion, whom he describes as "the vice-president and major stockholder of the film studio which just signed me."

Alexandra enters, looking for Chance. She realizes that his comeback has been a failure as was her own, and she wants to tell him that she actually feels some-thing for him in her jaded heart. She pleads with him to come away with her, but Chance scarcely hears her. Boss Finley's party arrives, and, for a long instant, Chance and Heavenly are suddenly standing face to face. Chance is stunned when she goes to join her father on the platform and when Tom Junior tells him about the operation Heavenly underwent after Chance passed a disease along to her on his last visit to St. Cloud. Boss Finley's voice booms out over the cocktail lounge television set. The heckler interrupts Boss's harangue on "purity of blood," but is quickly silenced, dragged into darkness and beaten, while a burst of applause is heard from the ballroom. Heav-enly leaves the ballroom, sobbing.

Later that night, in her hotel bedroom, Alexandra puts in one of several calls to the hotel operator for a driver. The act of calling for someone and getting no response has been repeated several times in the play: Boss's unanswered bellows for Heavenly from his terrace while she lies on the beach "like a dead body washed up on it," Chance's numerous telephone calls to Heavenly, all intercepted by Boss's servants, and a voice paging Chance Wayne for Alexandra during most of the scene in the bar.

Tom Junior and his henchmen push their way into the bedroom and conduct a fruitless search for Chance. They advise Alexandra to leave, since she has been traveling with a "criminal degenerate." After they leave, Chance enters from the gallery. Again Alexandra offers to take him away and save whatever traces of charm and sweetness are left in him. Chance's only response is to put in a long-distance call to Sally Powers, Hollywood columnist and close friend of Alexandra. He wants Alexandra to say that she has discovered a pair of new stars. Instead, Alexandra is thrilled to learn that her comeback picture was considered a triumph of mature artistry and has broken box-office records. She begins planning a week in a clinic, new photographs, and publicity. Yet she seems to understand that she does not have a clear progression of triumphs ahead of her.

For the last time, Alexandra asks Chance to leave with her. Both share a moment's realization that time is running out on them. Tom Junior comes to the door with a driver for Alexandra. She leaves. Chance remains, perhaps hoping that if Tom Junior carries out the long-standing threat of castration, a purification will result through his suffering a loss similar to the one he had inflicted on Heavenly. As the men move in for the attack, Chance steps forward to address the audience: "I don't ask for your pity, but just for your understanding—not even that—no. Just for your recognition of me in you, and the enemy, time, in us all."

*Sweet Bird of Youth* is not as good a play as Williams's other major works. Williams admits that in its construction he made the mistake of deviating from a straight line of narrative. That is, Act 2 features Boss Finley, the heckler, Miss Lucy, and Aunt Nonnie, all of whose motivations are underdeveloped. They distract from the more interesting relationship between Chance and Alexandra.

Boss Finley masquerades as a savior who heard the Voice of God in his youth, but he is evil incarnate. He has none of the vulgar charm of Big Daddy. In an interview with Lewis Funks and John E. Booth (*Theatre Arts*, June 1962), Williams admitted: "I have to understand the characters in my play in order to write about them because if I just hate them I can't write about them. That's why Boss Finley wasn't right in *Sweet Bird of Youth*, because I just don't like the guy, and I just had to make a *tour de force* of his part in the play."

Nor does there seem to be much redeeming virtue in the protagonist, Chance Wayne. Even his devotion to Heavenly is suspect, since he did nothing to help her when he learned of the disease he carried. Ironically, it is in giving up hope of fulfilling his youthful dreams that Chance finally attains a kind of dignity. He, unlike Boss Finley, progresses to an awareness of how far he has fallen from grace, and, despite his extreme degeneracy, one is surprised—as is Alexandra Del Lago in Act 2—to find that one can still feel something in one's heart for him.

*Sweet Bird of Youth* began as a one-act play which Williams decided to try out at George Keathley's Studio M Playhouse in Coral Gables, Florida. Austrian actress Margrit Wyler was engaged to play Ariadne (as Alexandra was then called). Encouraged by the enthusiastic cast during the rehearsal period, Williams continued rewriting until the piece turned into a three-act play. It opened as a work-in-progress on April 16, 1956.

Further revised, the play had its Broadway premiere on March 10, 1959. The critics were very favorably disposed toward Elia Kazan's direction, Jo Mielziner's settings, and the music by Paul Bowles. The play itself was regarded with a mixture of shock and fascination, and was hailed as one of Williams's finest dramas. Geraldine Page was praised for her trumpet-voiced bravura interpretation of Alexandra, a contrast to her characteristically soft-spoken manner.

Robert Coleman (*New York Daily News*) described Paul Newman's Chance as "a small-town hot-shot who hasn't the stuff to be a big shot. His disintegration when he finally faces up to reality has genuine emotional impact. Newman, as well as the audience, was moved by the concluding passage of the play. There were tears in his eyes as well as in those of many out front." Others in the cast were Sidney Blackmer as Boss Finley, Rip Torn as Tom Junior, Diana Hyland as Heavenly, Bruce Dern as the bartender, and Madeleine Sherwood as Miss Lucy.

Page, Newman, Torn, and Sherwood repeated their roles for the 1962 film version, which distorted the play by using numerous flashbacks and by bowdlerizing the ending. Chance is thoroughly beaten by Tom Junior, and his handsome face is smashed, but Heavenly arrives to give comfort and to depart with him from St. Cloud, while Aunt Nonnie rejoices for them. Richard Brooks thus directed what is almost a happy ending.

The Paris production of *Sweet Bird of Youth* featured the great classical actress Edwige Feuillère as Alexandra. Williams recalls in his *Memoirs* that "she was totally convincing and it was one of the great performances I've seen." The play was adapted for France by Françoise Sagan.

In 1975, *Sweet Bird of Youth* was staged at the

Kennedy Center in Washington, D.C., as part of a Bicentennial season of American drama. That production was taken to New York for a limited engagement at the Brooklyn Academy of Music, then moved to the Harkness Theater. Clive Barnes (*New York Times*) felt that "a lowering of voices perhaps, a concentration on theme rather than action—is perhaps the special grace of this new staging of the play by Edwin Sherin." The leading roles were played by Irene Worth and Christopher Walken.

## 28. Period of Adjustment

*Period of Adjustment* is a deceptively simple little suburban comedy that might have been written by any hack writer of situation comedy for television. The touch of the master lies in the details: the bemused treatment of middle-class American values, the wit, imagery, and natural rhythms of the dialogue, the liberal lacing of symbols, and dimensions of characters which echo Blanche, Kilroy, and others. The characters further belong to Williams in their strong preoccupation with sex. But they are "little" people, and, cosmically, their situation is trivial. Just as these characters would be scandalized by the elements of horror and depravity in Williams's other plays, their capacity to teach us about the human condition is limited. That this was deliberate on Williams's part is suggested in his essay "Prelude to a Comedy" (*New York Times*, November 6, 1960), in which he discusses the exhilaration of writing for its own sake as a kind of holiday from the writer's discipline of avoiding false intensities.

The action occurs in a suburb of a mid-Southern

city. Visible on stage are the front-entrance exterior of a Spanish-style stucco bungalow and the interiors of its living room and only bedroom. Beneath a large Christmas tree are a child's toys and a woman's fur coat. The play opens with a television commercial for a "new miracle product." It is watched by Ralph Bates, "one of those rare people that have the capacity of heart to truly *care*, and care deeply, about other people."

The sound of a car horn brings Ralph to the door, expecting to greet his old war buddy George Haverstick. Isabel, George's bride of thirty-six hours, comes up to the house while George parks the car. A few moments later, Ralph discovers that George has put all of Isabel's luggage on the doorstep and driven off. Isabel, already distraught because the marriage is not measuring up to her romantic fantasies, believes that George has abandoned her.

During the remainder of Act 1, Ralph and Isabel gradually reveal to each other what is wrong with their respective marriages. Ralph's wife of five years, Dorothea, had gone home to her parents that morning when Ralph told her that he had quit his stultifying job in her father's business. She took with her their young son who, Ralph believes, is being turned into a sissy. Their house in the suburb of High Point is built over an underground cavern, into which the entire suburb is slowly subsiding. The homeowners are keeping it a secret and selling out in alphabetical order.

"High Point over a Cavern," the subtitle of the play (or "High Point Is Built on a Cavern" in the acting edition), is a metaphor for Ralph and Dorothea's marriage—a materially respectable arrangement on a hollow foundation. Dorothea was a homely rich girl who was seeing a psychiatrist for "psychological frigidity" when Dorothea's elderly, ailing father held out to Ralph the possibility of inheriting the company if he would marry her. After marriage, Ralph cured Dorothea of her frigidity and became fond of her. This Christmas he had spent his entire savings on a fur coat for her, which now—on Christmas Eve—lies unclaimed beneath the tree.

Isabel met George when he was a patient at the St. Louis hospital where she was a student nurse. Ever since serving in Korea, George had been afflicted with a constant slight tremor, which aroused Isabel's sympathy. A small, delicate creature, she lost her job at the hospital when she fainted at the sight of blood. After their wedding the previous morning, they had set out on their honeymoon in a second-hand Cadillac funeral limousine. As soon as they were on their way, George told her that he had quit his job and that they might never return to St. Louis. The rest of their drive had passed in silence, broken only by disputes over the volume of the radio that played nothing but "White Christmas."

On their honeymoon night in the dreary Old Man River Motel, George approached her insensitively, and she ended up trying to sleep in a chair. Ralph now tries to assure Isabel that she and George are only going through a normal "period of adjustment." In his review of the Broadway production, Walter Kerr (*New York Herald Tribune*) remarked that "it's something of a wonder how the laughs get bigger each time the too-helpful phrase turns up."

Act 2 begins with the return of George, who had gone to buy a bottle of champagne for Ralph. George privately tells Ralph that he is ready to get rid of Isabel, the first woman who ever resisted his advances.

Ralph remembers from their wartime experiences that George's talk of female conquest is braggadocio. He makes several fruitless attempts to get George and Isabel together.

While Isabel is out walking Ralph's dog, George proposes that they find dignity for themselves in a bachelor existence together in West Texas—raising cattle for TV Westerns. When Ralph expresses reservations about George's "American dream," George calls him a "TV-watchin', canned-beer drinkin', Spanish-suburban-stucco-type son of—." Meanwhile, Isabel gets lost in the snow because there are five almost identical Spanish-type stucco cottages on the block.

Act 3 is enlivened by the arrival of Dorothea's parents, who have come with their maid to claim their daughter's valuables. When Mrs. McGillicuddy makes a sarcastic remark about "old wartime buddies," Isabel leaps to George's defense. Ralph tells off his stingy father-in-law. The McGillicuddies try to have Ralph arrested, but the police officer refuses "because of Mr. Bates having been a very well-known war hero." Dorothea enters, sends her parents away, and makes up with Ralph, although he suspects her of having come only for the fur coat. She tells him, however, that she knows all about the bargain Ralph made with her father, but she loves him anyway and is willing to go on with their marriage, always wondering if he loves her.

Dorothea invites the Haversticks to stay the night and use the sofa-bed in the living room. Dorothea borrows one of Isabel's honeymoon nightgowns, since Mrs. McGillicuddy had taken all of her clothes in the car. The two couples get ready for bed in the separate rooms, and the men tell their wives of the plans for a ranch in West Texas. The house rumbles and the ceiling cracks—a normal occurrence for this house built over a cavern. George admits his wedding-night nervousness to an understanding Isabel. The play ends on a note of tender reconciliation.

Some critics regard *Period of Adjustment* as a totally cynical black comedy. Certainly, the play has serious overtones, but if it is primarily a "social satire" of middle-class life, as Alvin Goldfarb suggests (in *Tennessee Williams: A Tribute*), it is compassionate rather than "stinging." Walter Kerr called it "quite honest social reporting with a faint ache behind it." Despite their limited vision and petty faults, the four main characters are good, likeable American people. The house's final tremor occurs only after Ralph and Dorothea have agreed to leave it together, so that their marriage is no longer tied to the house. The concluding stage picture of George and Isabel together before the glowing fireplace exploits the universality of the hearth as a symbol of shelter and domesticity.

*Period of Adjustment* was first produced at the Coconut Grove Playhouse in Miami on December 29, 1958. Two years later, on November 10, 1960, it opened in New York, directed by George Roy Hill. With some reservations, the reviews were generally favorable. Hill also directed the 1962 film version, which starred Jane Fonda and Tony Franciosa as Isabel and Ralph.

The London production opened June 13, 1962, and ran until November 3. The *London Times* reviewer enjoyed the honeymoon-farce aspects of the play, but regretted the "dogged and laborious underlining of an obvious moral" when attention is switched "to the more experienced husband's marriage."

A production in Hamburg, Germany, opened January 2, 1962, and was warmly received.

## 29. The Night of the Iguana

Looking back to 1962, it is now possible to confirm what was vaguely conjectured then—that *The Night of the Iguana* marked a turning point in Williams's work. According to an interview with Lewis Funke and John E. Booth (*Theatre Arts*, January 1962), it was written in a period of "spiritual exhaustion," and it seemed to be a mellow, reflective summation of many of his own "mixed feelings and attitudes." It even seemed possible that the absence in this play of Williams's characteristic concern with violence might adumbrate a new direction in his work. Williams has not, in fact, completely abandoned the subject of violence, but he has, since 1962, attempted a greater variety of styles and has tended to use a looser dramatic construction.

In that interview, Williams said that *"The Night of the Iguana* is a play whose theme, as closely as I can put it, is how to live beyond despair and still live." The solution that is found in the play for living beyond despair is to make human contact, to come out of one's "separate cubicle" and to experience compassion for other human beings, based upon acceptance.

The action occurs on the verandah of the Costa Verde Hotel, which is built in a tropical rain forest on a hilltop above the beach near Puerto Barrio, Mexico. It is the summer of 1940. Maxine Faulk, the proprietress, is a big, lusty woman with a short, barking laugh. She is delighted to see her old friend Shannon, Reverend T. Lawrence Shannon, who climbs up the jungle path and collapses, wild-eyed with fever, on her verandah. He has been conducting a Mexican tour for a busload of schoolteachers from Baptist Female College in Blowing Rock, Texas. But now he has departed from the tour itinerary, hoping that the ladies would appreciate the natural beauty of this spot while he spends a few days recuperating and talking to "cool and decent" old Fred, Maxine's husband.

Shannon's first setback is the news that Fred had died two weeks earlier. Maxine quickly makes it clear that she would like for Shannon to stay and take Fred's place. His second problem is the recalcitrance of the ladies on the tour, as exemplified by the "butch vocal teacher" Miss Judith Fellowes, who "comes chargin' up the hill like a bull elephant on the rampage." Shannon suspects that her long-distance telephone call from Maxine's office is an attempt to get him fired and to pin a charge of statutory rape on him. He tells Maxine that one of the tour members, Charlotte Goodall, a sixteen-year-old protégée of Miss Fellowes, has been throwing herself at him. Unable to cope any longer with this kind of problem, Shannon plans to go back into the Church. Maxine has, apparently, heard this before.

Miss Fellowes completes her call and stops to vent her mounting rage at Shannon. He pleads for her to understand that he is "a man at the end of his rope," but she hurls accusations about his conduct of the tour and drives him to the brink of hysteria with the culminating insult: "*De*-frocked! But still trying to pass himself off as a minister!" Maxine tells him to give up the bus key and let the tour go on without him, but Shannon does not want to lose this job as he has so many others, because there is nothing lower than Blake Tours.

Hannah Jelkes appears at the top of the path, pushing her "ninety-seven years *young*" grandfather Nonno, the well-known minor poet Jonathan Coffin. She is an ethereal yet androgynous-looking New England spinster in her late thirties. Maxine is doubtful about the pair's ability to pay and tries to turn them away, but Shannon intercedes for them. Maxine relents and gives Hannah and Nonno adjoining cubicles for one night. Shannon goes to the beach for a swim.

Several hours later, near sunset, Maxine asks to speak with Hannah while setting up folding tables on the verandah for dinner. Maxine has found a place in town that will take Hannah and Nonno on credit. Hannah tries to barter a piece of carved jade for additional time at the Costa Verde, but fails.

Four "Rubenesque" Germans are staying at the Costa Verde. Jubilant because of radio reports that London is on fire, they indulge in athletic horseplay and call for champagne. Charlotte Goodall comes looking for Shannon. Hannah tries to divert her, but Charlotte corners him and insists. "You've got to marry me, Larry, after what happened between us in Mexico City." After making love to her, he had struck her, then insisted that they pray together for forgiveness. He says, "I do that, I do that always when I, when . . . I don't have a dime left in my emotional back account—I can't write a check on it now." Upon the arrival of Miss Fellowes, Shannon runs into his cubicle and slams the door. Charlotte is dragged away, sobbing.

At the same moment, Shannon and Hannah step out onto the verandah to adjust their outfits: Shannon dons a black silk bib, a heavy gold cross, and a clerical collar; Hannah assumes her artist's smock with flowing silk tie. "They are like two actors in a play which is about to fold out on the road, preparing gravely for a performance which may be the last one." Shannon's intention is to show the ladies that he has not been defrocked as a minister of the Church.

Hannah asks him when and why he left the Church to become a tour conductor. Shannon tells his story while Hannah sketches a quick-character portrait of him. Only one year after his ordination, while serving as pastor to a wealthy congregation in Pleasant Valley, Virginia, he was visited in his study by a young Sunday-school teacher who declared her attraction to him. Shannon's response was to have her kneel and pray with him. But "the kneeling position turned to a reclining position on the rug of my study and . . . When we got up? I struck her. Yes, I did. I struck her in the face and called her a damned little tramp." The girl ran home and tried to commit suicide, thereby causing a scandal. The following Sunday, when he climbed into his pulpit and saw all the "smug, disapproving, accusing faces," Shannon threw away his apologetic prepared sermon and fulminated against Western theology's concept of God as an "angry, petulant old man," as a "senile delinquent." Shannon was then locked out of his church and sent to a private asylum to recuperate.

Since then, Shannon has been "collecting evidence" for his "personal idea of God, not as a senile delinquent," but as a God of Lightning and Thunder. Reacting to a sudden blazing shaft of golden light from sky to sea, Shannon exclaims, "That's him! There he is now! His oblivious Majesty . . ." Hannah expresses her belief that Shannon will go back to the Church and that, instead of giving a violent, furious sermon, he will see the faces "with eyes like a piercing cry for something to still look up to, something to still believe in," and he will "lead them beside still waters, because you know how badly they need the still waters, Mr. Shannon."

During their talk, Nonno's voice is heard from his cubicle, repeating lines of poetry. He is composing a new poem, his first one in twenty years. Maxine's two "Mexican concubines," Pancho and Pedro, arrive with an iguana they have caught. They tie it up under the verandah, so that after it is fattened up Maxine will have it to eat.

When the Germans return to the verandah for dinner, we see how Hannah and Nonno have supported themselves in their years of travel around the world. They pass among the tables and Hannah offers her watercolors and quick-character sketches for sale, while Nonno recites his poetry. But now, since Nonno seems to have had a slight stroke and cannot remember his verse, their efforts elicit no money from the Germans. Shannon settles Hannah and Nonno at a table and sees that they are served, despite the fact that—for the first time in all their travels—they are penniless.

Maxine wheels the liquor cart among the tables. She has been trying, since he arrived, to overpower Shannon in his struggle not to begin drinking. Shannon and Maxine fight, pushing the liquor cart back and forth between them like a battering ram, until Shannon runs off. Maxine then confronts Hannah. She says that she caught the vibrations between Hannah and Shannon, and she wants Hannah to "lay off" him. Hannah seems amused that she, a New England spinster, could be taken for a vamp. It is as if, like Alma and Blanche, Shannon were caught between a polarization of his physical and spiritual needs, embodied by Maxine and Hannah. Another basis for the compatibility of Shannon and Hannah may be detected in his assertion that he lives on the fantastic level but has "got to operate on the realistic level." To him, Hannah seems both to live and operate on the fantastic level; hence he is drawn to her.

When Shannon returns and sits at Hannah's table, Maxine's guarded reaction makes it clear that Hannah will definitely have to leave the next day. The theme of the play is restated in Hannah's and Shannon's ensuing conversation:

> SHANNON. Now I know why I came here!
> HANNAH. To meet someone who can light a match in the wind?
> SHANNON. To meet someone who wants to *help me*, Miss Jelkes.
> HANNAH. Has it been so long since anyone has wanted to help you, or have you just. . . .
> SHANNON. Have I—what?
> HANNAH. Just been so much involved with a struggle in yourself that you haven't noticed when people wanted to help you, the little they can? I know people torture each other many times like devils, but sometimes they do see and know each other, you know, and then, if they're decent, they do want to help each other all that they can. Now will you please help *me*? Take care of Nonno while I remove my watercolors from the annex verandah because the storm is coming up by leaps and bounds now.

Williams notes in the stage directions that "the storm, with its white convulsions of light, is like a giant white bird attacking the hilltop of the Costa Verde." And the dialogue concludes:

> HANNAH. . . . Here is your God, Mr. Shannon.
> SHANNON. Yes, I see him, I hear him, I know him. And if he doesn't know that I know him, let him strike me dead with a bolt of his lightning.

The act ends with a single shaft of light illuminating Shannon's hands, which reach up into the rain.

Several hours later, in the quiet, glistening tropical night after the storm, Shannon is seated at a table writing a letter to his former bishop. Maxine renews

her efforts to get Shannon to stay with her. She recalls
once overhearing Shannon telling Fred how his problems had started: his mother had invoked God's wrath
to make him feel guilty for any kind of sexual pleasure.
His experiences with young girls have been a way of
getting back at his mother. Maxine tells Shannon:
"We've both reached a point where we've got to settle
for something that works for us in our lives—even if it
isn't on the highest kind of level."

Shannon notices that his ladies are all gathered
around the bus. Jake Latta arrives, sent by Blake
Tours to take over Shannon's party. With the help of
the bus driver, Hank, Jake forcibly removes the bus
key from Shannon's pocket. Miss Fellowes takes her
last opportunity to humiliate Shannon, since she has
spent "this entire afternoon and over twenty dollars
checking up on this imposter with long-distance phone
calls." The irony is that Latta, into whose dirty, shaky
hands the ladies deliver themselves, is, as Shannon
calls him, a fat "degenerate, . . . this Jake Latta of the
gutter-rat Lattas."

Shannon admits that he took Charlotte "on a tour
of inspection of what lies under the public surface of
cities," as he apparently has done with young girls
several times in the past. But he defends himself in a
last, impassioned speech:

> I haven't stuck to the schedules of the brochures
> and I've always allowed the ones that were willing
> to see, to *see!*—the underworlds of all places, and
> if they had hearts to be touched, feelings to feel
> with, I gave them a priceless chance to feel and
> be touched. And none will ever forget it, none
> of them, ever, never!

This speech could be Williams's own answer to those
who have accused him of dwelling excessively upon

violence and degeneracy in his plays. We know that Latta and the ladies are the poorer for not being touched by it.

After a moment's pause, Shannon runs down the path toward the road. The sound of voices—shrieks and squeals of outrage—is heard. Then Shannon returns, so spent that he cannot remember what he has just done. When the sound of the departing bus motor tells him that his ladies are gone, he begins to pull at his gold cross on the chain around his neck. Hannah has observed the entire scene through the mosquito netting of her lighted cubicle. Only now, when she sees that the chain is cutting Shannon's neck, does she intervene. As soon as she unclasps the chain, he runs toward the beach to "take a long swim to China." Maxine sends her boys to catch him. They bring him back, struggling, and tie him in the hammock. While he is thus immobilized, the Germans gather around him and chuckle: "Is this true you make pee-pee all over the suitcases of the ladies from Texas? Hah? Hah? . . . Thees is vunderbar, vunderbar! Hah? Thees is a *epic gesture!* . . ."

Left alone with Hannah, Shannon asks her to untie him. She says she will, after he has calmed down, after he finishes indulging himself in his "Passion Play performance." Being tied in a hammock, she tells him, is an "almost voluptuous kind of crucifixion to suffer for the guilt of the world." She brews some mild, sedative poppyseed tea on her alcohol burner, because for all three of them—Shannon, her grandfather, and herself —"this won't be an easy night to get through."

Shannon manages to free himself and goes directly to the liquor cart, as if to provoke Hannah. But she tells him: "Liquor isn't your problem, Mr. Shannon." She says his problem is "the need to believe in something or someone." She has discovered that she can believe in communication between people outside their separate cubicles. She knows, further, that the only way to get through a crack-up, to beat one's private "spook," is by endurance.

Shannon asks Hannah if she has ever had any kind of a love life. Hannah, having said there would be no limit on questions and answers between them tonight, describes two love experiences she has had. The first occurred when she was sixteen: a young man in the Nantucket movie theater sat beside her and pressed his knee against hers. Her scream brought about the man's arrest, but she got him off by telling the police she was just overexcited by the Clara Bow picture. Her second experience occurred only two years ago, in Singapore. A traveling salesman took her out in a sampan and asked for an article of her underwear, which she gave him. Shannon asks if she wasn't disgusted by this sad, dirty little episode, and Hannah responds with the line that sums up her entire outlook: "Nothing human disgusts me unless it's unkind, violent."

This is a key to Shannon's uncharacteristic interest in a person other than himself. Because of Hannah's quasi-Oriental acceptance of things, she is not surprised or shocked at anything; she respects Shannon in spite of the unsavory aspects of his character she has observed. Shannon has never got close to other people because they could not see the decency of the idealistic self-image toward which he strove. He had always retaliated against this insensitivity by trying to shock and to provoke them: the heretical speech to his congregation; the side tours to show young girls the horrors of the city or tropical country they were visiting; his final gesture to the ladies from Texas; and even his challenge to God to strike him down with lightning.

He touches Hannah's throat, but she tells him to save it for the widow. He asks if they might travel together, but she realizes that this would not work. They are interrupted by the sound under the verandah of the iguana "at the end of its rope." Shannon makes the analogy: "Like *you*! Like *me*! Like Grandpa with his last poem!" Hannah asks him to cut the iguana loose, but he first tests her with a story of tropical squalor calculated to shock and disgust her. She reacts physically, but maintains her spiritual equanimity and reiterates her request.

As soon as the iguana, "one of God's creatures," is allowed to "scramble home safe and free," Nonno completes his poem. Hannah wheels Nonno out to the verandah, and he dictates to her his loveliest poem, a poem of acceptance:

> . . . Without a cry, without a prayer,
> With no betrayal of despair. . . .

Maxine enters, wearing her swimsuit. Shannon takes one last look at Hannah's face, which is briefly illuminated by a match. Then he follows Maxine to the beach and, evidently, into a permanent arrangement.

Nonno's head slumps to one side. Hannah discovers that he has stopped breathing. She almost panics. The final image of the play, as the curtain descends, is of Hannah's serene, loving acceptance.

*The Night of the Iguana* began as a short story published in *One Arm and Other Stories* in 1948. That story bears little resemblance to the full-length play that evolved from it over a thirteen-year period. In 1960 a one-act version was presented at the Festival of Two Worlds in Spoleto, Italy.

After a tryout on the road and several revisions, *The Night of the Iguana* opened in New York on

December 28, 1961. This important play was directed by Frank Corsaro and starred Bette Davis as Maxine, Patrick O'Neal as Shannon, and Margaret Leighton as Hannah Jelkes. The reviews were mixed. Descriptions of the play ranged from "searching, mystic, poetic" (*New York Daily News*) to "harrowing, unnecessarily sordid . . . repulsive" (*New York Mirror*).

John Huston directed the 1964 film of the same title. In updating the story, he eliminated the Nazis and placed more emphasis upon Miss Fellowes and Charlotte Goodall. Richard Burton, Deborah Kerr, and Ava Gardner were cast as Shannon, Hannah, and Maxine. Maurice Yacowar (*Tennessee Williams and Film*) feels that Huston's direction gave the film a "more robust spirit" than Williams had given the play, and made the film more comic as well as more positive.

The play was revived in New York at the Circle in the Square on December 16, 1976, with a production brought from the Ahmanson Theater in Los Angeles. *The Night of the Iguana* was now regarded as the last one of Williams's works that made much "sense" (*New York Daily News*) and as one containing elements that anticipated "the stylized, unreasonable plays to come" (*New York Post*). There were mixed reactions to Joseph Hardy's direction and to the cast, which included Richard Chamberlain as Shannon, Sylvia Miles as Maxine, and Dorothy McGuire as Hannah.

# III. LATER ONE-ACT PLAYS:
*Entering Dragon Country*

## 30. *In the Bar of a Tokyo Hotel*

The artistry of this short full-length play is decidedly subordinate to its importance as a compendium of Williams's preoccupations during the late 1960s. *In the Bar of a Tokyo Hotel* is an intellectually intriguing statement about the artist's conflicting relationships to his art and to his external reality, but it does not captivate either the heart, as do Williams's early plays, or the imagination, as do some of his other experimental works. Williams used this play as a stylistic test case for the incomplete sentence in stage dialogue. All four major characters speak lines like these:

> MIRIAM. Go back to the States. Enter a. Consult a. As your wife, I.
> MARK. I can't interrupt the.

Williams's fascination with the Oriental mystique —earlier manifested in Hannah Jelkes philosophy of acceptance and in the Kabuki scene—shifters in *The Milk Train Doesn't Stop Here Anymore*—culminates in his setting of this play in Tokyo, with a Japanese barman as an impassive foil to the highly charged American woman, Miriam. Miriam establishes herself as an aggressively masculine woman by smoking a pipe, by attempting to make an assignation with the barman, and, later, by hurling from her table a vase with its cut flower. She boasts of her own vital energy, which she contrasts with the apparent placidity of Oriental peoples and with the nervous collapse of her husband Mark, an established painter whose style is undergoing a "terrifying" and "uncontrollable" transition. Miriam fears only the effect of time upon her vitality. She intends to forestall any eventual decline in herself by taking a single pill which she carries with her.

Miriam cables Leonard, a gallery owner, asking him to fly to Tokyo and take Mark off her hands, so that she can continue her tour of Japan. Mark, unkempt in his paint-stained suit, stumbling and trembling, enters the bar and joins Miriam, ignoring her coldness toward him. She is tired of his "infantile dependence" on her. He raves about his experience of uncontrolled oneness with his art.

Mark pleads to accompany Miriam on her luncheon date, then accuses her—justifiably, it seems—of going to meet another man. She leaves. Mark remains at the table awaiting her return.

In Part 2, Leonard arrives from New York. He urges Miriam to minister to Mark's needs, but she callously refuses. Mark enters. He is out of breath, and his face is cut from shaving. Miriam again refuses him solace. He falls to the floor. With Mark dead, Miriam feels a release and an unexpected loss. She is suddenly without goal or vitality.

*In the Bar of a Tokyo Hotel* abounds with symbols; cut flowers, wind chimes, a Hawaiian lady crossing the room in the background, chiaroscuro effects. At the end, Miriam says that Mark made the mistake of deliberately moving out of the circle of light, that is, away from established norms. One might infer that he entered Dragon Country. Clearly, Mark expresses Williams's own artistic turmoil, while Miriam resembles the critics who refused to nurture the once-beloved artist.

The play was produced in New York at the Eastside Playhouse, directed by Herbert Machiz. It opened May 11, 1969, with Anne Meacham as Miriam, Donald Madden as Mark, and Lester Rawlins as Leonard. It closed after twenty-five performances. Devastated by reviews, which termed the play "therapy-by-confession" (Martin Gottfried, *Women's Wear Daily*) and "a cotton puffball of commonplace" (Clive Barnes, *New York Times*), Williams fled with Anne Meacham to Tokyo.

## 31. I Rise in Flame, Cried the Phoenix

This short dramatic tribute to D.H. Lawrence, written twenty-eight years before *In the Bar of a Tokyo Hotel*, is also about the death of an artist. Both D.H. Lawrence and Mark are debilitated and at the mercy of their dominating, sexually aggressive wives. Both are obsessed with light as one of the last imperishable forces.

Lawrence sits facing the sun on the porch of his villa in France. Weakened by tuberculosis, he knows his end is near. His wife Frieda accuses him of "sucking the fierce red sun in your body all day and turning it into venom to spew in my face!" Lawrence fears a loss of his intransigent masculinity, and he elicits a promise from Frieda that she will allow no woman to touch him while he is dying.

Their friend Bertha arrives. She is a tiny, virginal English gentlewoman. Her dialogue with Frieda points up her spiritual relationship with Lawrence in contrast to Frieda's physical one. Having just come from London, Bertha reports on the opening of an exhibit of Lawrence's paintings, which the critics called "disgusting," and that had caused a disturbance when a group of ladies attempted to slash a picture. Lawrence regards this as a triumph.

The sun begins to set. Lawrence comments, as he does every day, that the sun is being "seduced by the harlot of darkness":

> Now she has got him, they're copulating together! The sun is exhausted, the harlot has taken his strength and now she will start to destroy him. She's eating him up. . . . Oh, but he won't stay down. He'll climb back out of her belly and there will be light. In the end there will always be light —And I am the prophet of it!

Lawrence staggers to the window and collapses. Frieda restrains Bertha from rushing to him until he is dead.

The play makes the statement that, although women will suffocate his memory with their grief at his death, Lawrence will be reborn, like a phoenix, through his art. However, Williams's admiration for the works by Lawrence that helped to liberate sex from repression is tempered by his unsympathetic treatment of Lawrence as a man who both feared women and desired to master them.

According to Benjamin Nelson (*Tennessee Williams*), Williams had worked on this play as early as

1934, but was able to complete it only after his 1939 visit to Frieda Lawrence in Taos, New Mexico. It was not produced professionally until 1959, when it opened at the Theater de Lys in New York. In the ANTA company were Alfred Ryder, Viveca Lindfors, and Nan Martin.

## 32. The Mutilated

Williams's compassion for human outcasts is as sincere as ever in *The Mutilated*, but the play itself is too loosely constructed to win the traditional kind of audience involvement. At the same time, paradoxically, it is not experimental enough in comparison to *The Gnädiges Fräulein*, with which it was performed under the joint title *Slapstick Tragedy*. Set in the Silver Dollar Hotel in the French Quarter of New Orleans on Christmas Eve and Day, it offers a glimpse into the lives of two fiftyish floozies, Celeste Delacroix Griffin and Trinket Dugan, and the losers with whom they associate. A band of carollers intersperse the seven scenes with a song of hope for "the strange, the crazed, the queer," "the wayward and deformed," "the lonely and misfit," to whom a miracle is promised.

Celeste and Trinket have dissolved their friendship, since Celeste cruelly threatened to expose Trinket's secret. The mutilation about which Trinket is so sensitive is, apparently, a mastectomy. For three years now she has led a lonely existence without any male visitors to her room. Supported by her father's oil money, she could afford to leave the sordid environment, but she chooses to remain, continually dispensing tips and cheap gifts in hopes that some love will be forthcoming in return.

Celeste, just released from a stay in jail for shop-lifting, hopes to reinstate herself as a recipient of Trinket's generosity. When her first overtures fail, she resorts to scratching cruel remarks about Trinket's mutilation on the hotel walls. Celeste speaks the play's most telling line: "We all have our mutilations, some from birth, some from long before birth, and some from later in life, and some stay with us forever."

One of the latter kinds of mutilation is the loss of dignity, exemplified by the Bird-Girl that appears in one scene. This woman is paid to have chicken feathers stuck all over her skin with hot glue and to shuffle, flap, and croak as a freak attraction in the streets—a far cry from the charming mechanical bird-girl of *Eccentricities of a Nightingale*. The insensitivity of the hotel clerk, the cop, the habitués of the Cafe Boheme, and the sailor from whom Trinket tries to elicit some human warmth drives the two women to a reconciliation. While drinking California Tokay together in Trinket's room, they experience their miracle. They sense the invisible presence of Our Lady, the Virgin Mary, in the room. Downstairs in the lobby, Jack in Black enters, dressed in a rhinestone-studded cowboy outfit. His song indicates that he, Death, will temporarily suspend operations and smile upon the mutilated "for a while."

*Slapstick Tragedy*, which opened February 22, 1966, was attacked by most reviewers. *The Mutilated* fared somewhat better than its companion piece because of its clearer narrative. The performances of Kate Reid as Celeste and Margaret Leighton as Trinket were praised. Alan Schneider directed; Lee Hoiby composed the music.

## 33. I Can't Imagine Tomorrow

The title phrase "I can't imagine tomorrow," repeated three times in this short play, is a thematic statement: the play is about death. One, a woman, and Two, a man, are middle-aged characters, each the only friend of the other. Two makes his habitual evening visit to One's home, but they do not engage in their usual game of cards. One tells Two that "things have to change in life." One encourages Two to seek new friendships, and she asks him to leave when she goes upstairs to bed. Two closes the door, but remains. One accepts his continued presence.

The two characters' interaction is composed of rhythmically varied segments of pantomimic business and dialogue. Each of these interlocking sequences expresses a variation on the theme of the passage toward death. The simplest indications of stage action become disproportionately significant because of their symbolic overtones: the hesitation at the door, the closing of the curtains; Two's difficulty in completing a sentence; One's aversion to food.

Two tells of having applied for an opening with a therapist, whose receptionist could not fit him into the schedule. One later tells a parallel story about a little man that tried to enter the house of Death but was turned away because he was too early. Other key passages in the dialogue are One's speech about having seen a dark house with twenty white cranes stalking about on the lawn (souls in transit, one surmises) and One's speech about Dragon Country, "where there's no choice any more."

Death is desired by both characters One and Two, but for different reasons. Two is afraid of life. One wants something different from a life that offers only enervating sameness. Friendship is not a satisfying alternative to death, nor can a friend accompany one very far on the journey toward death; but friendship does prove to be, for One and Two, the most acceptable condition of life.

*I Can't Imagine Tomorrow* premiered on national television in December 1970, performed by Kim Stanley and William Redfield. It was produced for the stage by WPA Theater (Workshop of Players Art) in New York City during the 1974–75 season.

## 34. *The Frosted Glass Coffin*

This quick-sketch portrait of old age is set in front of a low-priced retirement hotel in downtown Miami. The title of the play refers to the white quality of the early-morning light on the scene, while a group of seventy- and eighty-year-olds waits on the sidewalk for the 7:30 A.M. opening of the cafeteria across the street.

One of Williams's insightful touches in the play is the apparently equal concern of his characters for a two-cent increase in the price of a bowl of cream of wheat at the cafeteria and for the sudden death during the night of one of their number. Commenting on the petty details of daily life and on eternal verities in the same breath, these characters possess dignity and stature far surpassing the magnitude of the play.

## 35. *The Gnädiges Fräulein*

Although it was either attacked or ignored by critics in their reviews of *Slapstick Tragedy* (the joint title for this play and *The Mutilated*), *The Gnädiges*

*Fräulein* is in Williams's own opinion his "best work of the sixties" (*Memoirs*). Margaret Leighton recognized in the play "a completely new departure for Tennessee," and Mike Steen saw it as "quite autobiographical in a more symbolic way" (*A Look at Tennessee Williams*).

The setting is the porch and picket-fenced yard of a dilapidated cottage on Cocaloony Key. The set and costumes are all in shades of "grays and grayish whites that you see in pelican feathers and clouds," except for the interior that is visible through the dirty net curtains of the window, and the costume of the Gnädiges Fräulein; these are vividly colored and evocative of another time and place.

Polly, the society editor of the Cocaloony Gazette, repeatedly crouches to dodge the overhead swooshes of cocaloony birds flying past, while she addresses the audience. She explains how the once-proud cocaloony birds have degenerated into parasites who live on the fish that are discarded by fish-boats as unfit for market. Polly joins Molly on the porch of the latter's rooming house. They sit side by side in rocking chairs, "synchronize rockers," smoke marijuana, and discuss Molly's lodgers.

One lodger is Indian Joe, a "blond Indian with Caribbean-blue eyes," an "erotic fantasy" with "a dancer's sense of presence and motion onstage." Another is the Gnädiges Fräulein, formerly an internationally celebrated singer, now a social derelict wearing the remnants of her theatrical wardrobe. She has fuzzy, bright-orange hair and, since this morning, a blood-stained bandage over one eye. Molly explains that the Gnädiges-Fräulein pays for her lodging with three fish a day. She competes with the cocaloonies for the throwaway catch, but today the birds turned against her and gouged out an eye.

During Molly's and Polly's conversation, a large cocaloony struts on stage, flaps, squawks, tries a rocking chair, exchanges monosyllables with Indian Joe, and suddenly flaps away. A fish-boat whistle is heard. The Gnädiges Fräulein dashes off with her bucket, her spirit unvanquished, to compete for the fish. When she returns, her tutu is spangled with fresh drops of blood, and she has lost her other eye. "However, her voice is clear and sweet as a bird's: I mean a songbird's. . . . She is transfigured as a saint under torture." Clearly, the Gnädiges Fräulein represents the indomitable spirit of the artist in the face of adversity and, more particularly, Williams's own perseverance despite critical hostility:

> POLLY. SHUT UP! SHE'S SINGING, GOD DAMN IT!
> MOLLY. I know she's singing! I didn't ask if she's singing. I asked is she out or in! (*Polly sings with her. The Fräulein stops singing.*)
> POLLY.—I think you scared her. She's quit.
> MOLLY. She always quits when somebody else chimes in, she will only sing solo.
> POLLY. Can't stand the competish?
> MOLLY. Yep. She's out again, now. I didn't want to look at her till my nerves was prepared for the shock of her appearance.
> POLLY. I think she's remarkable. I'm going to call her remarkable in the write-up.
> MOLLY. Don't overdo it.
> POLLY. Watch her: she's about to walk off the steps.
> MOLLY. She's gonna walk off the steps. She's gonna *nearly* walk off 'em: then stop short. —Intuition takes over when the faculties fail. I'm willing to make book on it.
> POLLY. She's shuffling along with caution.

168 | TENNESSEE WILLIAMS

MOLLY. Yep. That's what I told you.

POLLY. Look. She's stopped and set down. Let's shout bravo, applaud her, intuition or caution, she stopped at the edge of the steps.

MOLLY. Don't turn her head. I don't want self-satisfaction to become the cornerstone of her nature.

This and other transparent passages illustrate Williams's self-searching at the time. At the end of Scene 1, the Gnädiges Fräulein hears another fish-boat whistle and blindly rushes off with her bucket. Polly is lured inside by Indian Joe, while Molly, left on the porch, beats on the locked door.

In Scene 2, Polly returns to the porch, disheveled from her encounter with Indian Joe. Molly invites Polly to take notes on the Gnädiges Fräulein's background for use as a human interest story. The Fräulein was once part of a trained seal act that performed for the crowned heads of Europe. Its trainer was a Viennese dandy as handsome as Indian Joe. Hopelessly in love with him, the Fräulein tried to win him over by catching in her own teeth the fish that he tossed to the seal. Love thus provided the impulse for artistic creation.

When the Gnädiges Fräulein reenters, she is even more streaked with blood, and much of her orange hair has been torn away. But she has a fish in a skillet. Undetected by the blind Fräulein, Polly and Molly take the fish from the skillet and go inside. The Fräulein calls for "Toivo," the Viennese dandy. She senses Indian Joe's presence and offers him the supposed fish. He tells her that the skillet is empty and goes to join Molly and Polly at the dinner table. A fish-boat whistle again calls the Fräulein to her task.

The Gnädiges Fräulein is set apart from the other

characters by her bright color and by her willingness to sacrifice herself; she represents the true artist. Indian Joe, or the Viennese dandy, is a pseudo-artist selling his shallow external attributes. Taken in by these superficial appeals, Polly represents the media. Molly, who fancies herself a social leader, is proud of her contact with a "personage" such as the Gnädiges Fräulein, as long as the artist pays her way. Everyone comes in contact with cocaloonies, or whatever is unpleasant or disgusting in life, but only the artist is willing to grapple directly with them.

In the New York production of February 1966, Zoe Caldwell, Kate Reid, and Margaret Leighton played Polly, Molly, and the Gnädiges Fräulein respectively. All three were excellent, but Zoe Caldwell was singled out for special praise. John McClain (*New York Journal American*) wrote that the play "defies description. I haven't the foggiest idea of what Mr. Williams has to tell us, but it must be reported that it is extremely funny much of the time."

## 36. A Perfect Analysis Given by a Parrot

Bessie and Flora, the two middle-aged female clowns Williams created in Scene 5 of *The Rose Tattoo*, reappear in this 1958 playlet. Bessie is stout and Flora is thin, and both are loaded with bangles. In St. Louis for the National Convention of the Sons of Mars, they enter a tavern looking for some night life. They order beers and squeal with amusement as they recall the antics of the Sons of Mars at past conventions.

Flora mentions that she has had her character analyzed that afternoon. She paid a dime and a parrot gave her a piece of paper that read: "You have a

sensitive nature, and are frequently misunderstood by
your close companions." It gradually becomes apparent that, although both women are ridiculous,
Flora is not gratuitously cruel or vulgar, as is Bessie.
Bessie's remarks about Flora's appearance bring tears
from Flora, but the mood shifts abruptly back to
silliness with the leap-frogging entrance of two Sons
of Mars.

## 37. *The Demolition Downtown*

*The Demolition Downtown,* subtitled "Count
ten in Arabic—and try to run," was published in
*Esquire* (June 1971). In their upper-middle-class living
room, Mr. and Mrs. Lane discuss how they will continue to cope with living under the new revolutionary
regime, since they are running out of liquor and the
supermarkets are closed. Dynamite blasts periodically
rattle the windows and shake the pictures from the
walls. When the Lanes' two little girls arrive, having
escaped when their convent school was commandeered,
the parents' only reaction is to send them to bed.

Mr. and Mrs. Kane, friends of the Lanes, enter. The
fact that all of the friends they mention, even the ex-
President, have names that rhyme with theirs suggests
homogeneity of values and attitudes among the formerly "comfortable" classes. The two couples decide
that, combined, they have enough gas left to make it
to the mountains. The men go out to siphon gas and
oil from the Lane Mercedes into the Kane Caddy.
Hearing the Lane daughters sing the marching song of
the revolutionary forces, the two women realize that
in future they will be at the mercy of their children.
They devise a plan of their own: they put on plain
coats with nothing underneath, intending to offer

themselves to the revolutionary leaders downtown. They exit, singing the marching song. Their husbands enter and brush the plaster dust from each other's jackets.

In Spring 1978 Williams wrote an essay, "The Misunderstandings and Fears of an Artist's Revolt," published in *Where I Live,* which expresses the point of view that shaped this play: "No rational, grown-up artist deludes himself with the notion that his inherent, instinctive rejection of the ideologies of failed governments, or power-combines that mask themselves as governments, will in the least divert these monoliths from a fixed course toward the slag-heap remnants of once towering cities."

*The Demolition Downtown* was first produced at the Carnaby Street Theater, London, in January 1976, on a bill with *The Lady of Larkspur Lotion.* Irving Wardle (*The London Times,* January 13, 1976) found interesting comparisons between the two plays, written twenty-five years apart, about "evicting terrified victims from their place of residence." Whereas the Lady of the first play was a social derelict, *The Demolition Downtown* deals with the "hard middle-class majority who are experiencing the victim's role for the first time. . . . Nobody but Williams could have written the first of the two plays, but *The Demolition Downtown* might be the work of any capable scriptwriter."

# IV. LATER FULL-LENGTH PLAYS:
*Tilting at Windmills*

## 38. *The Milk Train Doesn't Stop Here Anymore*

Williams's account of the production history of *The Milk Train Doesn't Stop Here Anymore* in its several revised versions is intertwined, in his *Memoirs*, with his recollections of Frank Merlo's long terminal illness. Merlo, like Flora Goforth in the play, fiercely denied the inevitable approach of death. In fact, the play, first produced in 1962, almost seems to have anticipated Elisabeth Kubler-Ross's identification, in her 1969 book *On Death and Dying*, of "five different stages that a person will go through when he faces the fact of his own death: denial, anger, bargaining, depression, and acceptance." The play is a profound philosophical exploration of the nature of the experience that is the culmination of every human life, but it is not particularly good theater. It is one of very few instances in which Williams forgets to entertain his audiences even as he stimulates their emotional and intellectual awareness.

Two Japanese Kabuki-style Stage Assistants dressed in black serve throughout the play as scene shifters, moving screens to mask or unmask different playing areas: the library, bedroom, and terrace of Mrs. Flora

Goforth's white villa on an almost inaccessible mountaintop "above the oldest sea in the Western world," and the bedrooms of her nearby, smaller, pink and blue villinos. The Stage Assistants also help to remove the play one step from realism. They announce in the Prologue that the performance will cover "the two final days of Mrs. Goforth's existence."

The early scenes establish Mrs. Goforth as an enormously wealthy woman in her sixties, who has had four husbands, but has lately withdrawn from society. Her emblem, the griffin, represents her as a kind of human monster, like Alexandra Del Lago in *Sweet Bird of Youth*. While denying the fact that she has aged or changed at all, Mrs. Goforth dictates her memoirs under pressure from her publisher. She no longer eats, but seems to exist by means of drugs, pills, brandy, tape recordings of her own voice, and a bank of electric buzzers to summon servants. But when her doctor sends a portable X-ray machine, she pushes it off the terrace to crash on the surf-pounded rocks below. The boom of the waves under the mountain is a metaphor for eternity.

A young man, Chris Flanders, stumbles into the villa. Exhausted by the nearly impossible climb up the goatpath of Mrs. Goforth's mountain and wounded by her guard dog, he hands a servant a book of his own poems, *Meanings Known and Unknown*, to take to Mrs. Goforth. She appraises him through binoculars as a variety of summer freeloader, but gives orders to put him in the pink villino.

Before Chris falls asleep, he tells Mrs. Goforth's "Vassar-girl" secretary Blackie that he has had a good bit of experience with old dying ladies: "I've discovered it's possible to give them, at least to offer them, something closer to what they need than what they think they still want." He takes from his rucksack a mobile he has made, called "The Earth is a Wheel in a Great Big Gambling Casino," another gift for Mrs. Goforth.

The Witch of Capri, a fantastically robed matron, arrives in response to Mrs. Goforth's dinner invitation. Mrs. Goforth extracts information from her about Chris. She learns that Chris is well known in their social set, among whom he has earned the nickname "Angel of Death," because he has visited so many ladies shortly before their deaths. Together, they visit the villino where Chris is still asleep, and Mrs. Goforth removes the tray of food that was left for him.

Chris wakes up hungry in the night and wanders out to the terrace, where he is clubbed by Mrs. Goforth's sadistic watchman Rudy. Blackie rescues Chris. They go to her blue villino to talk, but they are almost immediately interrupted by Mrs. Goforth's buzzer. She dictates the story of her first husband's death, then staggers onto the terrace. Blackie reaches her just in time to prevent her from falling off the cliff.

The next morning Chris joins Mrs. Goforth for breakfast, but he still is given nothing to eat. Their long conversation in this scene contains much of the thought in the play, but neither character reaches any new understanding. Chris describes his need to have someone to care for, which he likens to the interdependence of two little puppies in a big, mysterious house. Mrs. Goforth, on the contrary, keeps an "oubliette," a little grass hut on the beach where she puts people away to be forgotten. She propositions him. Suddenly, she has a severe attack of coughing and bleeding. As Blackie helps her to her room, the servants begin snatching valuables.

Toward sundown of the same day, resplendent in

her finest jewels in order that they will not be stolen, Mrs. Goforth clings fiercely to life. She calls Chris into her bedroom and disrobes in an attempt to seduce him. He hangs the mobile he had brought and prepares to leave. She orders a meal for him, but still he resists her blandishments. He says that he tried to bring up the road something that would mean God to her, and he tells her what he has learned about "acceptance" of

> how to live and to die in a way that's more dignified than most of us know how to do it. And of how not to be frightened of not knowing what isn't meant to be known, acceptance of not knowing *anything* but the moment of still existing, until we stop existing—and acceptance of that moment, too.

Mrs. Goforth declares that she will "go forth alone," because she is not going to be a "milk train" for a freeloader. But a moment later she asks Chris to help her into her bed and not to leave her. The Stage Assistants hide them with a screen just as Chris begins removing her rings. Mrs. Goforth's flag is lowered. A bugle plays not Taps, but Reveille. Chris comes onto the terrace and tells Blackie that he put Mrs. Goforth's rings under her pillow "like a Pharaoh's breakfast waiting for the Pharaoh to wake up hungry. . . ."

In the 1959 short story "Man Bring This Up Road," on which *Milk Train* is based, Mrs. Goforth is treated as a kind of divine presence at the top of the mountain, with her three villas called Tre Amanti. She is not ill, but is merely allergic to something and she plans to have a specialist check every plant, animal, bird, and fish on the place. Her visitor, Jimmy Dobyne, climbs the mountain with his offering, his book of poems. He is encouraged to hope for food, but is given none, and he is finally sent back down the mountain, still hungry. If the story is an allegory of futile human efforts before a remote, implacable divinity, the allegory reversed itself in the play, the first version of which appeared in 1962.

Critics have suggested that Chris represents Christ, but it is more appropriate to associate him with St. Christopher, the patron saint of travelers, who bore the Christ child on his shoulders across the river. Chris, in the play, helps people make the crossing from life to death. Like Christ and all who come afterward, Mrs. Goforth will be resurrected to eternal life. Thus, the play's allegory is one of divine recognition of human effort or of help extended through a human intermediary.

*The Milk Train Doesn't Stop Here Anymore* might be seen as a modern version of *Everyman*. In the anonymous medieval morality play, Everyman is summoned by Death. He tries to cling to the things he valued in life, but is deserted on his journey by Fellowship, Kindred, Cousin, Goods, Beauty, Strength, Discretion, and Five Wits. Only Knowledge (Blackie, on Mrs. Goforth's journey) and Good Deeds (Chris) stay until the end.

The earliest dramatization of Williams's story was presented at the Festival of Two Worlds in Spoleto, Italy, opening July 11, 1962. Directed by Herbert Machiz, it featured Hermione Baddeley and Paul Roebling. Miss Baddeley later recalled (in *A Look at Tennessee Williams*) that they received "applause rather like the opera, you know. Ten, twelve, fifteen curtains. It was ecstatic." Williams own reaction was one of admiration for Miss Baddeley's talent.

These two leading performers were retained for the Broadway production, which had successful tryouts in

Boston and Philadelphia, but arrived in New York during a newspaper strike. The production opened January 10, 1963, and closed after sixty-nine performances. A revised version opened September 17, 1963, at the Barter Theater in Abingdon, Virginia. The Kabuki-style Stage Assistants were added at that time.

The second Broadway opening was on January 1, 1964. This production, directed by Tony Richardson, starred Tallulah Bankhead and Tab Hunter. Most critics did not appreciate the revisions. Walter Kerr (*New York Herald Tribune*) wrote: "The play has never really required more philosophizing. What it has wanted is some actual engagement between the people present, living and/or dead. No such source of tension, or involvement, or commitment, has been tapped. The boy revolves in an echoing outer space, without flesh. The woman drifts in her own vacuum." This version had only five performances in New York, but it was produced again by the San Francisco Actors' Workshop, directed by John Hancock, in July 1965.

A film version entitled *Boom* was released in May 1968. The casting of Elizabeth Taylor and Richard Burton eliminated the play's contrast between an older woman and a younger man, but pieced out Williams's philosophizing with a relationship between the two which fascinated millions during the actors' stormy union. Noel Coward played the Witch of Capri in this Joseph Losey–directed work. To most viewers the film is tedious and pretentious, but it has gained a cult following among those who agree with Maurice Yacowar's assessment in *Tennessee Williams and Film*: "This is the Williams film in which the characteristic resources of film—time, light, sound, color, the physical world of the settings, and the mythic world of the cast—are most fruitfully deployed."

## 39. Kingdom of Earth

The creative evolution of *Kingdom of Earth* spanned a twenty-year period, or thirty-five years if one traces it back to an incident which occurred during Williams's trip to Mexico in August 1940, when "perhaps the germ of [it] was first fecundated in my dramatic storehouse" (*Memoirs*). The short story "Kingdom of Earth" (published in *The Knightly Quest*) was written in 1954. A one-act play entitled *The Kingdom of Earth* was published in *Esquire* in February 1967. Under the title *The Seven Descents of Myrtle*, the expanded play—to which Williams refers in his *Memoirs* as "my funny melodrama"—opened in New York in 1968. In 1975 a revised and shortened script, retitled *Kingdom of Earth*, was produced by the McCarter Theater Company in Princeton, New Jersey; this latter version is the one published by New Directions, and the one discussed here.

It is not surprising, given its long gestation, that the play should combine themes from Williams's early and late periods. There is the familiar dichotomy of flesh and spirit, as represented by the two half-brothers. Occupying the kitchen during most of the play is Chicken, the dark-complexioned older brother who works in the fields and whose instincts are purely physical. He says: "You can't haul down your spiritual gates if you don't have any in you." Lot, the effete, consumptive, bleached-blond younger brother, abides in his mother's parlor with its gilt chairs and crystal chandelier or in his upstairs bedroom, sitting in a chair in the moonlight. Moving back and forth between the half-brothers is Myrtle, the bride who arrives home with Lot at the beginning of the play

Religious and sexual symbolism are both present in

references to the impending flood that threatens the Mississippi-farmhouse setting of the play. Lot married Myrtle, whom he picked up in Memphis, to keep the farm from going to Chicken when he dies of tuberculosis. Chicken was once turned off the farm by Lot's mother because he is one-eighth Negro. After his mother's death, Lot found that he was incapable of running the farm, and he lured his half-brother back to work on it by signing a legal paper that would leave the place to Chicken.

Myrtle apparently knew nothing about Chicken or about Lot's illness. She married Lot because he appealed to her maternal instinct. The story she tells about her long-ago loss of innocence is nearly identical to Bertha's tale in the one-act *Hello from Bertha.* Myrtle is vulgar, but warm, generous, and funny. Lot senses that he "won't see daylight again," and he sends Myrtle down to the kitchen to get Chicken drunk and then to retrieve the legal paper from his wallet. Myrtle periodically returns upstairs to minister to Lot, but with every descent she becomes clearly more attracted to Chicken.

Chicken manipulates Myrtle by threatening to let her drown with Lot in the flood. He has survived a previous flood on the roof of the house with the chickens, and he offers Myrtle that kind of salvation. Religious salvation he had once sought for himself and then rejected, because of the restrictions it placed upon his physical impulses. To Chicken, the only thing that matters is "what's able to happen between a man and a woman." Myrtle and Chicken become intimate, and afterwards, he tells her that he has "colored blood" in him. She is taken aback by this news, but it does not prevent her from accepting Chicken's invitation to "stay on here after Lot's gone," or—as she expresses it—to fulfill the "dream in her heart" of settling down "with a man to who she's very strongly attracted."

As Chicken and Myrtle arrive at their understanding, Lot is dressing up in his mother's clothes, a blond wig, gauzy white dress, and picture hat with faded flowers. He descends to the parlor, where he crumples to the floor. Chicken confirms that Lot is dead. Then there is the booming sound of the dike giving way. Chicken takes Myrtle to the roof as the curtain descends.

The theme of survival in the play may draw some of its immediacy from Wililams's own health problems in the mid-1960s. According to Mike Steen in *A Look at Tennessee Williams*:

> Tennessee told me that when he has Lot die, he is killing off all the wispy, willowy women he has written about, that he wasn't going to write that kind of woman anymore. Well, when Lot dies, Chicken, who represents all that is coarse and vulgar and hard, inherits the land—symbolically inherits the earth. He vindictively shouts, "Chicken is king!" Tennessee's viewpoint is the opposite of the biblical dictum that the meek shall inherit the earth. He has come to believe in the survival of the hardest.

Opening March 27, 1968, in New York as *The Seven Descents of Myrtle*, the play received mixed reviews. Although Clive Barnes (*New York Times*) identified "one of those highly charged Southern themes full of sex and other natural disasters," he and most other critics felt that the major interest of the play was in the characterization of Myrtle. That role was played by Estelle Parsons. She was supported by Harry Guardino as Chicken and Brian Bedford as Lot. The production was directed by José Quintero.

A film entitled *The Last of the Mobile Hot-shots* (1969), directed by Sidney Lumet, was based on *The Seven Descents of Myrtle*. In this version, the religious overtones were abandoned, and emphasis was placed upon the racial aspect by the casting of black actor Robert Hooks as Chicken. Lynn Redgrave played Myrtle, with James Coburn as her husband.

In 1978 the play was staged at the Mossoviet Theatre in Moscow under the title *The Knightly Quest*.

## 40. *Small Craft Warnings* and *Confessional*

*Small Craft Warnings* is an expanded version of the long one-act, *Confessional*, which is published in *Dragon Country*. The characters and much of the dialogue remains the same, even the spotlit confessional monologue of each habitué of the Southern California beachfront bar where the action occurs. *Small Craft Warnings* is a plotless, or "impressionistic," play, but it is important in Williams's canon for its two striking female characters, Leona and Violet.

Violet is a pale, fragile creature who looks as if she is made of "wet biscuit dough," or as if "the bones are dissolving in her." She has large, moist eyes and weeps easily. Leona sees her as a kind of water plant, because Violet seems to float, mentally and physically, from one temporary protector to another. She lives in a room without bath, over an amusement arcade where she meets sailors. Her most frequent companion is Steve, a forty-seven-year-old short-order cook who cannot afford to marry her, but buys her junk-food meals in exchange for her favors; he sees Violet as one of the "scraps in this world." Her fingernails are dirty, but "she's got some form of religion in her hands," because she goes into a trancelike state when she puts her hand under the table to feel the groin of any man within reach. Despite her degeneracy, Violet has a bizarre sort of beauty. Williams wrote in a letter published with *Small Craft Warnings* that perhaps his favorite character in *Confessional* was Violet.

In dramatic contrast to Violet is the central character of *Small Craft Warnings,* Leona Dawson, whom Williams has called "a fully integrated woman" (*Saturday Review*, April 29, 1972). "She is the first really whole woman I have ever created and my first wholly triumphant character. She is truly devoted to life, however lonely—whether it be with a stud like Bill or some young faggot she takes under her wing because he reminds her of her brother." Leona lives in her own trailer and pays her own way. She is a beautician, and she knows that she is good at her work. She is sensitive to beauty, whether she finds it in nature, in her grandmother's lace tablecloth and silverware, or in a sentimental violin piece she plays repeatedly on the jukebox in remembrance of her long-dead younger brother.

Leona has much compassion, but her own values are absolute. She tries to prevent the drunken "Doc" from delivering a baby illegally, but she offers to help young Bobby learn his way around the gay scene. In *Small Craft Warnings*, Violet says of Leona: "She's got two natures in her. Sometimes she couldn't be nicer. A minute later she. . . ." Twice during the play Leona chases Violet into the ladies' room where Violet retreats behind the locked door for self-protection.

Among the other characters is Monk, the owner-bartender. He takes a sincere personal interest in his regular customers. He is the "monk" who hears their confessions, and he himself "confesses" that they "take the place of a family in my life." All of the characters are "regulars" except Quentin and Bobby. Quentin, a jaded Hollywood screenwriter, had picked up Bobby on the road, but they soon separate, finding that they are uncomfortable together.

The action of the play could be any evening at Monk's Place, except for a few decisive acts by certain characters. In Act 2, Doc returns from his call to deliver a baby and confesses to Monk that the baby was born dead. While he was putting it in a shoe box and leaving it where the tide would take it, the mother began to hemorrhage. She died before Doc could bring himself to call an ambulance and incur the consequences of practicing medicine without a license. Now, Doc must hit the road tonight.

Leona, already tense because it is the anniversary of her brother's death day, becomes enraged when her lover, Bill, encourages Violet to fondle him under the table. She tells Bill to get his things out of her trailer, because she is ready to move on to a new town, a new beauty shop job, a new tavern with new acquaintances. And, finally, tonight, instead of walking back to her apartment over the amusement arcade with Steve, Violet goes up the stairs to Monk's apartment. Monk has told her to take a shower, and the sound of the water is symbolic of the cleaning of the soul through confession.

Several aspects of *Small Craft Warnings* recall the major plays of Williams's favorite dramatist, Anton Chekhov, who wrote that "people eat their dinners, just eat their dinners, and all the time their happiness is being established or their lives are broken up." So it happens in *Small Craft Warnings* while people just drink their drinks. As in Chekhov's plays, psychological interaction builds up to the moment of a departure, with its stamp of finality upon developing relationships. Despite the shabbiness of Williams's characters' lives, they command interest because Williams, like Chekhov, has found much that is lovable and funny about them. We are all, of course, like these characters, small craft on the sea of life. There is a vague feeling of hope and uplift at the end of the play when Monk switches off the lights and opens the door for a moment to the booming sound of the ocean, before he goes upstairs to join Violet.

*Confessional* was produced in summer 1971 at Bar Harbor, Maine. Its favorable reception prompted Williams to expand it into *Small Craft Warnings.* This allowed for fuller development of the characters, several of whom are among the best Williams has created since *The Night of the Iguana.* The longer version, directed by Richard Altman, opened April 2, 1972, at the Truck and Warehouse Theater in New York. The production was later moved to the New Theater. As a means of increasing attendance, Williams himself took the role of Doc; this was his acting debut.

In January 1973, *Small Craft Warnings* was produced at the Hampstead Theater Club in London. Elaine Stritch played Leona, and Irving Wardle (*The Times,* January 30, 1973) called it "her best part so far on the London stage."

## 41. *Out Cry* and *The Two-Character Play*

Many twentieth-century playwrights have dramatized man's ability to exist on various levels of reality and illusion. Some—for example, Luigi Pirandello in *Six Characters in Search of an Author,* Jean Genet in *The Balcony* and *The Blacks,* Jean Anouilh in *The Rehearsal*, Peter Weiss in *Marat/Sade*—have expressed it in terms of life versus theater. Although Williams has always used theatrical devices to transcend realism, his *Out Cry* and *The Two-Character Play* mark his first full-scale use of the play-within-a play technique.

Critics have objected to the obscurity in these two plays, but the fault cannot be ascribed to their structure, which is not unusually experimental, either in the context of Williams's dramaturgical development or in the broader context of modern drama. One may safely say that Williams's primary purpose was to make a personal statement about the artist in society. That statement may indeed be so personal as to mar the theatrical effectiveness of the work, but *Out Cry* and *The Two-Character Play* have, at least, a more lyrical texture than other contemporary dramatic expressions in this mode.

The earliest version of this work, entitled *The Two-Character Play*, was produced in London in 1967. A revision entitled *Out Cry* was presented in Chicago in 1971. Further revised, it opened in New York as *Out Cry*, in March 1973, and was published by New Directions in the same year. The most recent text is the one published as *The Two-Character Play* in volume 5 of *The Theatre of Tennessee Williams*. That version, produced off-Broadway in 1975, is the one discussed here.

The setting for the play-within-the-play is the sunny interior of a living room in the Southern town of New Bethesda. There are Victorian furnishings, tokens of the vocation of an astrologer, a door, and a window through which tall sunflowers can be seen. Surrounding this stage setting is the backstage clutter of a theater in an unknown, "frozen country." The latter area suggests not only "the disordered images of a mind approaching collapse but also . . . the true world with all its dismaying shapes and shadows." This outer reality, in contrast to the warmly lit interior setting, is dark and cold.

The two characters in both the play and the play-within-the-play are Felice and Clare, a brother and sister whose names mean "happy" and "bright," respectively. They are an actor and actress, and Felice is also a playwright, author of "The Two-Character Play" which they perform within *The Two-Character Play*. Felice is the more intense and sensitive of the two; he is an artist groping for fulfillment.

In *Out Cry*, Clare is very much like Felice, representing perhaps the feminine side of the artist's nature or else the muse that inspires the artist to create, as did Williams's own sister Rose. In *The Two-Character Play*, Clare's real-life personality is coarsened: her manner alternates between grand theatricalism and vulgarity. It is only in the role of Clare in Felice's play that she becomes childlike and pure. Williams may have strengthened Clare's frame-story character as a reaction to critics' unfavorable comments about the interchangeability of the two characters. The change might be explained as an indication of the occasional balkiness of the muse, since Clare in *The Two-Character Play* frequently opposes Felice's creative will. She also serves as a reminder that no artist can afford to neglect the practical business aspects of his or her work.

Clare sweeps into the theater expecting a press reception, but instead Felice shows her a cablegram from the rest of their company that reads: "Your sister and you are insane. Having received no pay since . . . we've borrowed and begged enough money to return to . . ." Clare, exhausted from their long travels, wishes to cancel the performance. Since there is an audience out front, Felice insists that they perform "The Two-Character Play," even though only part of the set has arrived. Felice tells Clare: "Tonight there'll be a lot of improvisation, but if we're both lost in the play, the bits of improvisation won't matter at all, in fact they may make the play better."

The performance begins with a discussion of their situation—living in a house in which the telephone and electricity have been disconnected. Clare's bedroom is the one in which their father, an astrologer, killed their frigid, domineering mother and then shot himself. Clare had wandered sleeplessly about the house the night before until she found a long-lost ring with her birthstone, the opal, a stone with "a sinister reputation." Felice touches the ring on her finger— "a sort of lovemaking"—but she strikes a note on the piano as a signal that she wants the sequence cut short.

They seem to return to reality momentarily when they notice the cablegram from the company on the set. Felice crumples it and throws it out the window. They reimmerse themselves in the world of the play and focus upon another symbol, the sunflower. Felice describes a brilliant, golden, two-headed one in the front yard that has grown as tall as the two-story house. Clare sees this as a monster of nature rather than as a marvel, but Felice defends nature's aberrations. An analogy of the artist as an aberration in society is implicit: "My opinion is that nature is tolerant of and sometimes favorable to these— differentiations if they're—usable?—constructive?— But if you're not, watch out you!"

Since there is no stage crew to knock on the door, Felice raps several times on the piano lid. Clare pantomimes picking up a card supposedly slipped under the door. The card is from "Citizens' Relief." The pair's reaction to this possible source of aid is one of fear and suspicion. Felice and Clare have been too long isolated from the world. They have scarcely left the house since their parents' murder/suicide, because they fear the gossip and hostility of local people, who regard them as deranged. Felice urges Clare to go out and call upon people. Instead, she uses the telephone, which we know to be disconnected, and engages in a long conversation with Reverend Wiley.

Felice uses a "prohibited word": "confined." For him and Clare, as for any artist, confinement is the condition most to be feared. It is the condition Williams experienced when he was committed to the hospital in St. Louis for three months in 1969, and it is the central metaphor of the play-within-the-play. Felice and Clare become furious with one another. He tries to suffocate her with a sofa pillow. They break apart and announce an intermission.

Act 2 of both plays opens with a new symbol: soap bubbles. As children, Felice and Clare blew soap bubbles on the back steps: that is, the act of artistic creation was spontaneous. But now, their activity is confined to the parlor. Felice warns that "soap bubbles floating out of the parlor window would not indicate to the world that we were in full possession of our senses."

They consider going out of the house to Grossman's Market, since they can get no more deliveries on credit. Clare is afraid of encountering some vicious boys who once scrawled an obscene word on their back fence. Inside the house, however, she fears her father's revolver, which Felice has hidden. We now learn that Felice was once confined in a mental hospital. He tells Clare that they must go out or else give up "all but one possible thing." The "one possible thing" might be interpreted as either incest or death.

In preparing to go out, the two characters, or actors,

seem to mock their own performance. Felice pushes Clare out the door and he follows. She is overcome by her fear and runs back inside. He follows. He is supposed to try to drag her out while she clings to the newel post of the stairs, but since the stair unit is not on the set, they begin to narrate their stage business. Felice declares that he and Clare must not live together in the same house any longer if they are unable to go out. He threatens never to come back. He goes out the door, but stops, facing the audience.

FELICE. . . . I feel so exposed, so cold. And behind me I feel the house. It seems to be breathing a faint, warm breath on my back. I feel it the way you feel a loved person standing close behind you. Yes, I'm already defeated. The house is so old, so faded, so warm that, yes, it seems to be breathing. It seems to be whispering to me: "You can't go away. Give up. Come in and stay." Such a *gentle* command! What do I do? Naturally I obey. [*He turns and enters by the door.*] I come back into the house, very quietly. I don't look at my sister.

CLARE. We're ashamed to look at each other. We're ashamed of having retreated—surrendered so quickly.

FELICE. There is a pause, a silence, our eyes avoiding each other's.

CLARE. Guiltily.

FELICE. No rock hits the house. No insults and obsenities are shouted.

CLARE. The afternoon light.

FELICE. Yes, the afternoon light is unbelievably golden on the—

CLARE. The furniture which is so much older than we are—

FELICE. I realize now, that the house has turned to a prison.

> CLARE. I know it's a prison, too, but it's one that isn't strange to us.

The sequence suggests the loneliness of the artist in charting a new course, and the overwhelming temptation to turn back to the comfort of his own past, proven work.

Felice finds the revolver and loads it. Clare nervously tries to divert him.

> FELICE. . . . I put the revolver in the center of the little table across which we had discussed the attitude of nature toward its creatures that are regarded as *unnatural* creatures, and then I— [*After placing the revolver on the table, he pauses.*]
> CLARE. What do you do next? Do you remember?
> FELICE. Yes, I— [*He starts the tape recorder.*] —I pick up my spool and dip it in the water and blow a soap bubble out the parlor window without the slightest concern about what neighbors may think. Of course, sometimes the soap bubble bursts before it rises, but this time please imagine you see it rising through gold light, above the gold sunflower heads.

Suddenly, Clare stops the performance. She tells Felice that the audience—whom she calls "the favorites of nature," that is, the well-integrated members of society—has left; the theater is empty.

Clare wonders if "The Two-Character Play" ever had an ending. This is another manifestation of Williams's recurring theme of incompletion. She says that "the worst thing that's disappeared from our lives is being aware of what's going *on* in our lives." Felice goes off to call for a hotel reservation. There are distant sounds of running footsteps and clanging metal.

Felice returns to break the news that all of the buildings' doors are locked from the outside, that there are no windows, and that the backstage phone is as dead as the prop phone in the play.

The extreme cold causes Clare's mind to wander. Felice suggests that they go back into the play, in which the imagined summer and light will make them warm again. They take off their coats. Clare tells Felice to put the cablegram back on the sofa. This is a wonderfully Pirandellian touch in that it forces us to call into question all our earlier assumptions about the divisions between reality and performance in *The Two-Character Play*.

They start from the beginning and, in a dozen lines, reach the climax of their play. Clare tells Felice to look out the window at the brilliant, giant sunflower. She picks up the revolver and aims it at him. He says harshly: "Do it while you still can!" She cries, "I can't!," and drops the revolver. Felice then picks it up and tries to shoot her, but cannot. Their faces admit defeat. They slowly embrace as the lights dim out.

In the earlier version, *Out Cry*, there is more emphasis on fear as a controlling force. Felice and Clare are already on the verge of hysteria when they make their first entrances. Their fears are symbolized by a towering, dark statue that cannot be pushed offstage. It figures much more prominently in their consciousness than does the statue of a giant among the backstage clutter in *The Two-Character Play*. Only "unalterable circumstances" seem to force Clare and Felice to overcome their fear in *Out Cry* and to accept their situation. The last line of the play is: "Magic is the habit of our existence." They stand motionless and accept the fading of the lights "as a death, somehow transcended."

*The Two-Character Play* is one of Williams's major works. Superficially, it appears to be very spare and abstract, approaching the styles of Samuel Beckett or Harold Pinter, both of whom Williams admires. References in the play to such matters as the murder/suicide, neighbors who throw stones at the house, and the revolver, all are tantalizing hints at a conventional stage action that never materializes. The work succeeds in the way Chekhov finally succeeded, with his last play *The Cherry Orchard*, in ending a complex drama for the first time without resorting to a revolver shot. Close examination of the play will reveal the rich texture and intricate patterns within the work. The play has not yet found general acceptance in the theater, but it may need something like the seventeen-year gestation that *Camino Real* had before audiences caught up with it.

*Out Cry*, the version that opened March 1, 1973, at the Lyceum Theater in New York, starred Michael York and Cara Duff-MacCormick. It was directed by Peter Glenville.

# V. WORKS IN PROGRESS: AN EPILOGUE

Tennessee Williams still considers himself a playwright-in-progress, whose art is continually developing. That he still cares deeply about polishing and perfecting each play is reflected in the fact that, at this writing, he has not yet deemed ready for publication several already-produced plays. Among these is *The Red Devil Battery Sign*, which is set in Dallas shortly after the assassination of President Kennedy. A production directed by Edwin Sherin and starring Anthony Quinn, Claire Bloom, and Katy Jurado opened in Boston on June 18, 1975. It closed ten days later. A revised version was produced at the English Theater in Vienna, Austria, opening January 18, 1976. Sy Kahn's review of the latter production appears in *Tennessee Williams: A Tribute*.

*This Is (An Entertainment)* premiered at the American Conservatory Theater, San Francisco, on January 20, 1976. This "exotic comedy" is set in a luxury hotel in a small European country on the eve of a revolution. Williams was present for rewriting during rehearsals and during part of the eleven-week run. The production was well supported by the public, but it failed to find favor with local critics.

*Vieux Carré* was Williams's first play since *The Night of the Iguana* to open on Broadway. It opened May 11, 1977 in a production that was widely discredited for its "desultory" (Brendan Gill, *The New Yorker*) and "inept" (T.E. Kalem, *Time*) direction, a "painfully trashy set" (Martin Gottfried, *New York Post*), and "downright amateurish lighting" (Howard Kissel, *Women's Wear Daily*). Sylvia Sidney was praised for her performance as Mrs. Wire, a New Orleans French Quarter rooming-house landlady. The narrator/protagonist is The Writer, whose involvement with other tenants is based upon Williams's own experience in the late 1930s.

*Tiger Tail*, a play based upon the characters and situation in the film *Baby Doll*, had its world premiere at the Alliance Theater in Atlanta in January 1978.

The June 1978 Spoleto USA Festival in Charleston was the occasion for the world premier of *Crève Coeur*. The title means "heartbreak" and also refers to an amusement park area outside St. Louis in the mid-1930s. This tender and funny play features a cast of four women. Revised, expanded, and retitled *A Lovely Sunday for Crève Coeur*, the play had a limited engagement at the Hudson Guild Theatre in New York in January and February 1979.

It is said that Williams keeps a trunkful of plays in progress. Some of these that have been mentioned in the press are: *Whore of Babylon* (or *Edible, Very*), *The Latter Day of an Aging Soubrette, Stopped Rocking* (a television play), *Serafina* (a musical version of *The Rose Tattoo*). In addition, there is an unpublished play, written in 1960 and dedicated to Yukio Mishima: *The Day on Which a Man Dies: an Occidental Noh Play*. The manuscript is deposited in the

UCLA Research Library. That library and the Humanities Research Center in Austin, Texas, house important collections of Williams's manuscripts.

*The Tennessee Williams Newsletter,* beginning publication in 1979 under the editorship of Stephen S. Stanton of the University of Michigan, is evidence of Williams's assuredly preeminent place in American letters. Walter Kerr *(New York Times,* May 22, 1977) eloquently expresses what underlies the current reawakening of popular appreciation for Tennessee Williams's work:

> Tennessee Williams's voice is the most distinctively poetic, the most idiosyncratically moving, and at the same time the most firmly dramatic to have come the American theater's way—ever. No point in calling the man our best living playwright. He is our best playwright, and let qualifications go hang. In fact, he has already given us such a substantial body of successful work that there is really no need to continue demanding· that he live up to himself, that he produce more, more, more, and all masterpieces. We could take some casuals and just tuck them into the portfolio, gratefully, as small dividends.

# BIBLIOGRAPHY

WORKS BY WILLIAMS

*Plays*

*American Blues: Five Short Plays* (*Moony's Kid Don't Cry; The Dark Room; The Case of the Crushed Petunias; The Long Stay Cut Short; or, The Unsatisfactory Supper; Ten Blocks on the Camino Real*). New York: Dramatists Play Service, 1948.

*At Liberty*, in *American Scenes*, William Kozlenko, ed. New York: John Day Co., 1941.

*Baby Doll* (the script for the film, with the two one-act plays that suggested it, *27 Wagons Full of Cotton* and *The Long Stay Cut Short; or, The Unsatisfactory Supper*). New York: New Directions, 1956.

*Cat on a Hot Tin Roof* (with revisions made for the American Shakespeare Theater production). New York: New Directions, 1975.

*The Demolition Downtown. Esquire* (June 1971), 124, 126–7, 152.

*Dragon Country* (*In the Bar of a Tokyo Hotel; I Rise in Flame, Cried the Phoenix; The Mutilated; I Can't Imagine Tomorrow; Confessional; The Frosted Glass Coffin; The Gnädiges Fräulein; A Perfect Analysis Given by a Parrot*). New York: New Direction, 1970.

*The Theatre of Tennessee Williams*, Vol. I (*Battle of Angels, The Glass Menagerie, A Streetcar Named Desire*). New York: New Directions, 1971.

————, Vol. II (*The Eccentricities of a Nightingale, Summer and Smoke, The Rose Tattoo, Camino Real*). New York: New Directions, 1971.

————, Vol. III (*Cat on a Hot Tin Roof, Orpheus Descending, Suddenly Last Summer*). New York: New Directions, 1971.

————, Vol. IV (*Sweet Bird of Youth, Period of Adjustment, The Night of the Iguana*). New York: New Directions, 1972.

————, Vol. V (*The Milk Train Doesn't Stop Here Anymore, Kingdom of Earth, Small Craft Warnings, The Two-Character Play*). New York: New Directions, 1976.

*Twenty-seven Wagons Full of Cotton and Other Plays* (*27 Wagons Full of Cotton; The Purification; The Lady of Larkspur Lotion; The Last of My Solid Gold Watches; Portrait of a Madonna; Auto-Da-Fé; Lord Byron's Love Letter; The Strangest Kind of Romance; The Long Goodbye; Hello from Bertha; This Property Is Condemned; Talk to Me Like the Rain . . .; Something Unspoken*). New York: New Directions, 1966.

*Out Cry*. New York: New Directions, 1969.

*You Touched Me!*, with Donald Windham. New York: Samuel French, 1947.

*Poetry and Prose*

*Androgyne, Mon Amour*. New York: New Directions, 1977.

*Eight Mortal Ladies Possessed*. New York: New Directions, 1974.

*Hard Candy and Other Stories*. New York: New Directions, 1967.

*In the Winter of Cities*. New York: New Directions, 1964.

*The Knightly Quest and Other Stories*. New York: New Directions, 1966.

*Memoirs*. Garden City, N.Y.: Doubleday and Co., 1975.

*Moise and the World of Reason*. New York: Simon and Schuster, 1975.

*One Arm and Other Stories*. New York: New Directions, 1950.

*The Roman Spring of Mrs. Stone*. New York: New Directions, 1950.

*Where I Live; Selected Essays*. New York: New Directions, 1978.


WORKS ABOUT WILLIAMS

*Books*

Donahue, Francis. *The Dramatic World of Tennessee Williams*. New York: Frederick Ungar Publishing Co., 1964.

Falk, Signi. *Tennessee Williams*. Boston: Twayne Publishers, Second Edition, 1978.

Fedder, Norman J. *The Influence of D.H. Lawrence on Tennessee Williams*. The Hague: Mouton and Co., 1966.

Jackson, Esther Merle. *The Broken World of Tennessee Williams*. Madison: The University of Wisconsin Press, 1966.

Leavitt, Richard F. *The World of Tennessee Williams*. New York: G.P. Putnam's Sons, 1978.

Maxwell, Gilbert. *Tennessee Williams and Friends*. Cleveland and New York: The World Publishing Co., 1965.

Miller, Jordan Y., ed. *Twentieth Century Interpretations of A Streetcar Named Desire*. Englewood Cliffs, N.J.: Prentice-Hall, 1971.

Nelson, Benjamin. *Tennessee Williams; The Man and His Work*. New York: Ivan Obolensky, 1961.

Stanton, Stephen S. *Tennessee Williams: A Collection of Critical Essays*. Englewood Cliffs, N.J.: Prentice-Hall, 1977.

Steen, Mike. *A Look at Tennessee Williams*. New York: Hawthorn Books, 1969.

Tharpe, Jac, ed. *Tennessee Williams; A Tribute*. Jackson: University of Mississippi Press, 1977.

Tischler, Nancy M. *Tennessee Williams: Rebellious Puritan*. New York: Citadel Press, 1961.

Tischler Nancy M. *Tennessee Williams*. Austin, Texas: Steck-Vaughn Co. (Southern Writers Series). 1969.

Weales, Gerald. *Tennessee Williams*. Minneapolis: University of Minnesota Press (Pamphlets on American Writers, No. 53), 1965.

Williams, Edwina Dakin (as told to Lucy Freeman). *Remember Me to Tom*. New York: G.P. Putnam's Sons, 1963.

Windham, Donald, ed. *Tennessee Williams' Letters to Donald Windham 1940–1965*. New York: Holt, Rinehart, Winston, 1977.

Yacowar, Maurice. *Tennessee Williams and Film*. New York: Frederick Ungar Publishing Co., Inc., 1977.

*Articles*

"The Angel of the Odd." *Time* 79, no. 10 (March 9, 1962), 53–60.

Brown, Dennis. "Miss Edwina Under Glass." *St. Louisan* 9 (March 1977), 59–63.

Buckley, Tom. "Tennessee Williams Survives." *Atlantic Monthly* (November 1970), 98–108. Williams's reply, *Atlantic Monthly* (January 1971), 34.

Evans, Oliver. "A Pleasant Evening with Yukio Mishima." *Esquire* 77 (May 1972), 126–30, 174–80.

Funke, Lewis, and John E. Booth. "Williams on Williams." *Theatre Arts* 46 (January 1962), 17–19, 72–73.

Gaines, Jim. "A Talk about Life and Style with Tennessee Williams." *Saturday Review* 55 (April 29, 1972), 25–29.

Heilman, Robert Bechtold. "Tennessee Williams," in *The Iceman, the Arsonist, and the Troubled Agent.* Seattle: University of Washington Press, 1973.

Kalson, Albert E. "Tennessee Williams Enters Dragon Country." *Modern Drama.* 16 (June 1973), 61–67.

Kazan, Elia. "Notebook for *A Streetcar Named Desire*" in *Directors on Directing,* Toby Cole and Helen Krich Chinoy, eds. New York: The Bobbs-Merrill Co., 1963, 364–369.

Magrid, Marion. "The Innocence of Tennessee Williams." *Commentary* 35 (January 1963), 34–43.

Phillips, Gene D. "Tennessee Williams and the Jesuits." *America* (June 25, 1977), 564–65.

Stanley, Williams T., comp. "Tennessee Williams," in *Broadway in the West End; An Index of American Theatre in London, 1950–1975.* London: Greenwood Press, 1978.

Vidal, Gore. "Selected Memories of the Glorious Bird and the Golden Age." *New York Review of Books* (February 5, 1976), 13–18.

Williams, Tennessee. "We Are All Dissenters Now." *Harper's Bazaar* 105 (January 1972), 40–41.

# INDEX